C000162630

EXPOSED...

God's Love Revealed

SHAWNA MARTIN

Exposed...God's Love Revealed
Trilogy Christian Publishers A Wholly Owned Subsidiary of Trinity Broadcasting Network 2442 Michelle Drive Tustin, CA 92780

This book is a memoir. All of the events written are true to the best of the author's memory and experiences. It is not the intent of the author to hurt or harm any person with the publication of this book and only shares that which is necessary and relevant to the story. No names have been used to protect the parties involved. Any information contained is not intended as a substitution for professional legal, financial or medical advice. Do not use this information to diagnose or develop a treatment plan without consulting a qualified healthcare provider. The author is not directly affiliated with, nor represents or necessarily shares the views of any organization, business or product mentioned herein. The author takes no responsibility for any individual interpretation or application of the content written in this book.

10 9 8 7 6 5 4 3 2 1
Library of Congress Cataloging-in-Publication Data is available.
ISBN: 979-8-89041-328-4 | E-ISBN: 979-8-89041-329-1

DEDICATION

This is dedicated to all those who feel or have ever felt lost, alone or unloved.

I thank God and His Word for graciously guiding me into His truth. "I am the way and the truth and the life" (John 14:6, NIV).

To all of my family and friends who have supported and encouraged the manifestation of God's will in my life.

I want to thank my best friend, Mike, who became my safe place in this world. For spending years helping me rebuild my self-esteem, believing in my dreams and giving me the courage to become the woman I was meant to be. Most importantly, for teaching me that laughter fixes almost anything.

I would like to personally thank Joyce Meyer for obeying the call on her life and inspiring me to keep pressing on.

Contents

PREFACE

"May the God of hope fill you with all joy and
peace as you trust in him, so that you may overflow
with hope by the power of the Holy Spirit"
(Romans 15:13, NIV).

Ever since I was a young girl, I remember battling intense feelings of depression, anxiety and suicidal thoughts well into adulthood, but in the fall of 2010, I fell into a very deep pit. I can still remember the day I felt the presence of gloom and doom come upon me. It ended up being a very dark and scary place, and I ended up fighting for my life for the entire next year. Day after dreary day, I was filled with hopelessness, fear and discontent. I had four very active teenagers at home, a stressful office job, and an emotionally unsupportive husband, all of whom I was trying not to let down. I felt like I was at the end of my rope most days and barely hanging on. I was too scared to share my feelings with anyone for fear of being invalidated or judged for not just being happy or a stronger person. But I was most afraid to be left alone, fearing that the thoughts I struggled with would cause me to harm myself as a way to escape from the pain. It was too hard to live, but I didn't want to die, even though much of the time, I felt like dying was the only way out. I only remember everything was covered in complete darkness; my mind, my life and my future.

From the outside, it appeared that all was fine. I looked like I had a successful career at a reputable company making good money, four healthy and beautiful children and a faithful husband who loved and adored me. We had a beautiful home plus a seasonal vacation spot at a popular campground in Northern Michigan. However, inside my mind, I was in the pit of despair. I wanted to be happy and grateful for all the blessings I had, but instead, I felt trapped, overwhelmed and exhausted just trying to keep up with all the demands of daily life. I would often ask myself, why can't I just be happy? Everybody else has responsibilities to deal with, so why couldn't I be content with mine?

I finally realized only one of two things could happen: I could either get better or I could just get worse. I decided during the midst of this incredibly daunting season, which I felt would never end, that I would have to really strive to find the light again, but I decided I would do whatever it took to get there. Due to my desperation to find answers, I read and listened to every resource that seemed to offer any sort of help or explanation for what I was going through. I had such an insatiable appetite for knowledge and answers that I devoured anything I could get my hands on. One day, a friend of mine from church gave me a bunch of Joyce Meyer's tapes. There were so many that I had to put them all in a duffle bag. Then, I put the bag in my minivan and would just insert one after another into the tape player. I wouldn't even look at the titles of each tape before putting the next one in, yet, every message seemed to be divinely inspired to give me exactly what I needed to hear at the perfect time. I started to realize that God was near, that He was listening to my cries for help and that He knew the pain I was experiencing in my heart and mind. And most importantly, that He was rescuing me, one moment at a time. I was also reading any inspirational or faith-based book that crossed my path, which I have listed at the end of this book as recommendations, depending on your situation.

One day, while I was still struggling with this deep state of depression, I met with one of my aunts at a local coffee shop. This is the same aunt who led me into a personal relationship with Jesus Christ when I was a young girl. Well, I guess some of the information and revelations I had been learning in my search for answers came out of my mouth because, at one point, she stopped the conversation and stated in all seriousness that she foresaw me writing a book. My instant response was to rebuke the idea. I immediately thought, what would I have to share that anybody would want to read about, or what new information could I bring forth since every subject known to mankind has already been written about? Plus, I had never thought of or desired to write a book. In fact, I was still trying to figure out my purpose in life. Well, as it turns out, God must have agreed with her or actually had given her that word of knowledge because it came true shortly thereafter.

Two weeks later, as I was turning down the blankets to go to bed, suddenly, the book title *Exposed...God's Love Revealed* came to my mind out of nowhere. I didn't think much of it as my husband and I went to bed as normal. As soon as I awoke the next morning, several chapter titles started downloading into my mind. I quickly grabbed a pen and paper and started writing as fast as my hand could move, making sure I got them all down. There were nineteen chapters in total, and I had listed them all in chronological order as they came to me. Filled with a glimmer of hope and excitement, I got on my computer and immediately started writing in these chapters for the next four days. I was filled with so much divine inspiration that I was typing stories and scriptures, including many scriptures I didn't realize I even knew. I was so thrilled to have renewed hope, believing that God did have a purpose and plan for my life. I thought this was it! My dreams of doing something great for God had finally arrived. Then, just as quickly as the Holy Spirit had come, He was gone.

I didn't have any more words or ideas to write about. I tried coming up with more material in my own effort, but it was fruitless. It was like waking up from a dream before it was finished. I then became worried that it was all just my imagination and was nothing of real significance. I thought maybe I had gone crazy or had some kind of manic episode. That was until I took a closer look at what I had written and realized that many of the chapters God had given me, I had not even lived through yet. I am not sure which is crazier, to see a prophecy be fulfilled or to see how your life will unfold into prophetic chapters not yet fulfilled. Over the next seven years, I watched as my life unfolded into each of these chapters. The awareness of this book was always in the back of my mind, so I got pretty good at recognizing which chapter I was living in as the seasons of my life changed. I was shocked, and sometimes saddened, that many of the chapters did not turn out the way I expected or hoped they would. And some chapters I feared going through were not as bad as I had thought they would be. But God has always gotten me through each one and safely onto the next. This reminds me that His grace is truly enough.

After all the years of patiently waiting with hopeful expectation for this book to be completed, God never let the dream die, no matter how long it took. The apostle Paul reminds us in Philippians 1:6 to be confident that He who has begun a good work in you will be faithful to complete it. I believe that God is the author and finisher of our lives, and everything works out in His perfect timing. For even when my mind doubted, or my circumstances showed otherwise, my heart chose to believe that someday, God would bring to fruition all these dreams that I had tucked away in my heart.

In 2018, the time had finally come to write the book. Looking back, I can see how all of my experiences, heartbreaks, and disappointments led me to seek more knowledge, which produced more wisdom and, ultimately, this amazing story of hope and healing. My desire is to reveal to you the greatest love story of all time, the one that Jesus Christ died for us to know. I don't know if we can ever fully comprehend His love for us and the power of the Holy Spirit within us until the day we see Him face to face in all His true glory, but there is no reason we can't try to grasp it while we are here.

At the end of each chapter, you will find bullet points to help you apply useful strategies to find victory in your own life, a prayer request from my heart concerning you and a declaration of His promise for you to claim for yourself. Remember, prayer is the simple act of communicating with God, and we can trust that He hears us and will answer us. Hebrews 4:16 tells us to come boldly to the throne of grace, that we shall receive mercy and grace in our time of need. The declaration is for you to speak out loud. We are told in Proverbs 18:21 that life and death are in the power of our tongue, and we shall eat of its fruit, so I encourage you to speak the truth of God's Word over your life and your loved ones, regardless of what the situation appears to be. I hope that you will be encouraged, inspired and forever changed by reading my story of hope and healing.

Prayer: *I pray that the messages contained in this book will fill you with faith, hope and love as God reveals His perfect love and redemptive plans for your life. Amen.*

Declaration: *The Lord has good plans for me, to prosper me and not to harm me, to give me a future and a hope (Jeremiah 29:11).*

CHAPTER 1

A Loss Of Innocence

*"Since you were precious in My sight, You have
been honored, And I have loved you"
(Isaiah 43:4, NKJV).*

I was a happy, healthy baby girl born in June of 1978, which was the year of the great blizzard in Michigan. Thankfully, this was now summer, and my family survived, even me in the womb of my mother. I was always a good little girl who loved everyone around me, and they all loved me. I believe at a young age I even knew that God was real and loved me. I actually accepted Jesus Christ as my Savior when I was just seven years old. I remember that moment like it was yesterday, at the local gas station while my aunt was filling up her gas tank. I guess you could say I was filling up my spiritual tank.

It was on a cold, blistery winter day in January and was actually my mother's birthday. It was just me and Jesus in the front seat of my aunt's car. Now, a gas station wouldn't be thought of as a holy place; it's not very clean and reeks of gasoline fumes. It was not your typical, spiritual place like a church or during a home Bible study. It reminds me of how Jesus was born in a dirty, smelly barn surrounded by farm animals on a cold winter's day. It doesn't seem right that the God of the universe would choose not to come into the world in a more majestic place of honor like a palace or maybe Holiday Inn. It just shows the nature of God, who loves to break into the middle of all our filthy messes to cleanse us from right where we are or where we have been.

I am so grateful that God captivated my heart at a young age before my years of chaos and rebellion started due to all the pain and suffering I would experience from living in a broken and fallen world. At the young age of only four years old, I started having dreams that were sexual in nature. I can still remember how vivid and perverse some of them were. There was some speculation that things may have happened to me when I was just a baby, but nobody knew for sure. I asked many times over the years if anybody had seen or known anything until, finally, I got an answer. I was forty-four years old when one of my uncles confessed that he had sexual intercourse with me when I was about four years old.

However, the first sexual encounter that I actually do remember was when I was in elementary school. My mom had to go out, I assume, for work, so she had one of my older cousins watch my brother and me for the evening. He was in his twenties and offered to let me stay up later if I would let him touch my private area as he brushed his hand between my legs. I remember the uneasiness and fear I felt at that moment as I pulled all of my stuffed animals close to me as if somehow they would protect me. Thankfully, he accepted no for an answer and left my room. Already at such a young age, I felt some kind of shame or embarrassment since I did not tell my mother or anybody else about it until a few years later. I wonder, what makes me and other sexual assault victims feel like we must keep these violations a secret when we didn't do anything wrong? Regardless, I somehow fell for the lie that it would be easier for me to carry the burden of guilt and shame than to hold them responsible for their actions, which would be the shame I ended up carrying for several more decades.

As I got older and started developing physically, sexual harassment just became the norm for me. From being whistled at by older men while walking down the street to having guys gawk at me with their lustful eyes at the store. On a few occasions, I barely escaped untouched. One evening, as a young teenager, I was visiting a cousin who lived a few hours away, and I went to use her restroom. A male friend of hers followed me into the bathroom and held the door shut so I couldn't get out. I don't know what he intended to do, but I told him that I would scream if he didn't let me out, and so he did.

Another time, I spent the night at another cousin's house, and when everybody went to bed, I stayed up to watch television. As I was sitting on the floor, I accidentally hit the power button on the remote control, and the television went off. It instantly went dark in the room, and I could not get it to turn back on. An older man in his twenties, who had been sitting on the couch, came up behind me and started kissing me on my legs. I was so scared but managed to muster up the courage to tell him that if he did not leave me alone, I would scream and wake everybody up. Thankfully, he left me alone the rest of the night. Unfortunately, not all these situations did I end up so lucky.

When I was in middle school, my friends and I had the normal girls' night slumber party. There were four of us who spent the night together at one of my best friend's houses. We all had our sleeping bags and pillows laid out for our campout on the living room floor. We had a great time with lots of laughter and stayed up late. As a rule of thumb and typical at most sleepovers, whoever fell asleep first is subjected to pranks. Of course, that would have been me. I fell asleep before the other girls, so they had fun writing all over my arms and legs with lipstick and markers. I eventually woke up before they went to sleep, and their chuckles clued me into what they had done.

When we finally went to bed, we all slept with our sleeping bags positioned so that our heads were in the middle of the room together. There was a young man, again in his early twenties, who was staying in the home. My friends hung around him a bit and talked to him throughout the evening, but I stayed away from him. Due to my past situations, I was very leary of older men. In the middle of the night, I awoke to my sleeping bag unzipped, and he was doing things of a sexual nature to me. At first, I was paralyzed in fear. I quickly realized what was happening but didn't know how to react. I was too scared to say anything or scream, so I pretended that I was still sleeping and squirmed around until he left me alone. He finally gave up and went away.

The next morning, I was up before anybody else, so I locked myself in the bathroom. I stayed in there until I heard somebody else get up. I then came out and saw my friend's mom and asked if that man had left. She found that to be an odd question and realized something was wrong, so she got me to tell her what happened. Thankfully, because I did tell her, it was reported to the police. After some time on the run, he was arrested, served time in jail and is now registered as a sex offender. Hopefully, by pressing charges, he never sexually assaulted anybody again.

Of course, it would be apparent why I did not trust

men, especially older men. I was full of fear and tried to avoid them, if at all possible. But you cannot stay away from them all, especially when one of them is someone you've known since birth and was supposed to be able to trust with your whole life. It was summer break just before sixth grade, and I was staying with my dad and my grandma for the summer. I had my own bedroom, and one night, after I went to sleep, I was awakened by the sound of my dad coming into my room and crawling into my bed. When I was younger, he would typically give me a back massage or hug and kiss goodnight but this time was different as I felt his hands under my pajama top and bottoms.

Just as I had experienced in the past, I was so startled and scared that I could not scream or say anything. I just pretended that I was sleeping and squirmed around to get into another position so that he could not touch me anymore. Eventually, he got up and left my room. The next day, I did not say anything to anybody. My dad was gone to work, and I was home alone with my grandma. My stomach was nauseous at the realization of what had happened the night before. I thought I was going to vomit but somehow contained myself. I didn't even cry; I think I was in shock. I never told anybody for quite a few years and managed to act like everything was normal. I kept all the pain, shame and humiliation inside to protect myself and him.

From that moment, I always made sure my younger brother was with me when I had to spend nights at my dad's house. I would sleep with one eye open, wondering if his desire for me would come back. Thankfully, if that urge ever did come back, he never acted on it again. I think one of the worst things a little girl can go through is to have her daddy fall that hard off the pedestal she had him on. My dad was supposed to be my protector, not another predator. He was supposed to be the one man whom I could trust to guard me against all the other men who tried doing that very same thing. Now, I was just as afraid of him as all the other men.

Back in my younger years, one of my favorite movies was *Grease*. There was a scene where one of the girls told her friend that the only man a girl could trust was her daddy. That statement never settled well with me again. I loved watching the TV show *Full House*. The daughters were close to their dad and would hug him or sit on his lap, and I would just cringe because I wanted to warn them to be careful. I was waiting for him to touch them like my dad did to me. I even remember worrying for years, afraid that my stepdad would come into my room some night, but he never did. I just expected all men to be the same.

For years, I wondered what I did to entice all these

men. I couldn't remember doing anything specifically to warrant their advances. Most of these men I had never talked to before, and I certainly would not try to seduce my own father. Plus, I was just a child. But I still thought something was wrong with me or that I had done something wrong. I figured I must be to blame for some of this. By the time I was thirteen years old, I was smoking cigarettes, sneaking out of my bedroom window with my boyfriend most nights and started being sexually active. I was insecure, angry and rebellious. I did not feel close to my parents nor trust many other adults. Even though I lived in fear of older men, I was very comfortable with boys my own age. I gained an attraction for the bad boys, who gave me the attention I desired, as well as a sense of security from all the other men.

The effects of childhood sexual abuse continued well into my forties, as I was still vulnerable to the sexual harassment and coercive behaviors of men. It has been a very long journey of learning to value myself, demand respect and not feel obligated to say yes when I really want to say no. To this day, I have a very hard time trusting people, especially men. But God reminds me that He is near to me, protecting me and that I no longer have to fear the consequences of speaking up and enforcing healthy boundaries. I know the layers of healing will continue, but I also believe that I will continue getting stronger as I lean into God's perfect love for me.

Life Lessons

- Nobody ever deserves to be sexually assaulted, abused or raped. You always have the right to say no.
- Anybody who has to coerce or manipulate you into doing things that you do not feel comfortable with is a violation of your personal boundaries.
- You have the right to say no to anyone at any time without the fear of abuse, punishment or retribution.
- If you have ever been or know someone who has been sexually assaulted, please tell someone you trust or seek professional counsel.
- Some people who sexually violate another person do not have only one victim. Seeking criminal charges for sexual abuse may not only bring justice for you but could prevent it from happening to another.
- I know the effects of sexual assault can often leave the victims feeling like they did something wrong. Sexual abuse is not the victim's fault.
- If you have ever been the victim of a sexual assault, please know that you are not damaged, devalued or worthless.

Prayer: *Lord, I pray that You heal anyone who has ever been a victim of sexual abuse and remind them that they are loved and valued. Amen.*

Declaration: *I know that I am fearfully and wonderfully made (Psalm 139:14).*

CHAPTER 2

HATED WITHOUT A CAUSE

"And his banner over me was love"
(Song of Solomon 2:4, KJV)

My parents were separated and divorced when I was just four years old. It wasn't until I was going into sixth grade that they each started seriously dating someone else and eventually remarried. Everybody got along with each other to the extent that holidays and family occasions were celebrated harmoniously together, even with exes and new spouses in attendance. That may seem socially unorthodox, but it was better for me as a child to see everyone getting along rather than holding onto resentments due to failed marriages. Parents separating or divorcing is already hard enough for a child to go through without any added strife and animosity.

Of course, this didn't happen immediately, but it took a few years to get to this point. I was grateful that I always had much family around who loved me, even if it was blended. Everybody seemed to work together to share the burdens of raising us children, hence the statement that it takes a village. This lifestyle allowed me to find some contentment and stability, even with my past abuses. However, it didn't stay this way forever.

I don't know exactly when or why things turned around or what I did to seem to be the cause of it. I was about sixteen when I started opening up about what my dad had done several years earlier, and at some point, my stepmom began to despise me. I don't know what I did wrong, but whatever it was made her very upset. For years, she had called me her daughter, but now I was her enemy. Not only was it hard for me but the whole family to have this hatred interjected into it. I was confused, angry and could not understand why she rejected me when I thought she loved me.

Now, I admit that at this time, I was a full-blown teenager with the cocky, rebellious attitude that comes with that age. However, I don't recall being so horrible as to receive this degree of treatment. It has been speculated that much of her resentment toward me had to do with what my dad did to me, but I cannot confirm this. I don't know if she believed that the incident was my fault or that I could have prevented it in any way, but she had questioned another family member about why I didn't stop my dad. Regardless, there was always something she would find to be angry with me about.

One of the most confusing aspects was that in one moment, she would be nice to me, and in the next, she would be furious at me again. There seemed to be no real reason any of us were aware of for her to constantly target me as the source of her anger. One of the hardest parts to deal with was that my dad didn't know how to protect me from her wrath, nor did my family, so they really didn't. Her attacks were very unpredictable, and she could turn on me at any time for any reason. And because she was the type that could only extremely love or extremely hate anyone, nobody wanted to end up on her bad side. Something as simple as not agreeing or believing in the same things as she did would get you cut off.

In order for my dad to live at peace with her, he basically had to take her side most of the time. This became the case with the rest of my family, as well, and I was no longer invited to the family's birthday parties or gatherings because nobody wanted to upset her. I never understood how she gained so much power and control over my family or how anybody could think I deserved this indignation. I assume they all just wanted peace, and it must have been easier to quietly push me aside. This unfair treatment of being the outcast that started as a young teenager continued well into my twenties. My dad and stepmom ended up having a son together, and I was apparently on her good side the day she gave birth because I was there for the delivery. Of course, that was short-lived. Eventually, nobody could mention my name in her presence for fear of her anger. But sometimes, my dad would sneak my stepsister and half-brother over to see me.

One day, I found out there was a birthday party for my dad at my grandpa's house. The whole family was there, but I was not even told about it. Well, I showed up in my pajamas, hysterical and in tears. I am pretty sure I told my family exactly what I thought about what they had allowed her to do all of these years. I then sent a letter to my step-mom that cursed her every way but sideways and proba-bly that way, too. It was the final straw; I was filled with so much bitterness and resentment that I unleashed every unkind word I could think of and told her exactly where I thought she should go. It wasn't my finest hour, but I was still young and consumed with so much hurt and pain after years of rejection and betrayal.

By my mid-twenties, my stepmom gave my dad the ultimatum to disown me or divorce her. He chose to leave her. I was grateful that he finally chose me; however, it just ended up being one more thing I blamed myself for. A few years later, when God had started me on my healing jour-ney, I was walking through a local convenience store when a song came on, and the letter I had sent to my stepmom came to my mind. I was immediately convicted and even saddened by the words I had written. I felt led by the Holy Spirit to write a letter of apology and to take back all the curses I had said over her. So, I did just as I believed God had told me to. Then I asked Him if I had to send it. His instant reply was, "Well, you sent the first one." Of course, my heart sank in fear, but I knew what I had to do.

I wrote a heartfelt apology for all of the pain I had caused her and for the horrible letter I had sent a few years prior. I was nervous, not knowing what her response would be, if any. But I trusted God's plan. Within a few days, I received an email from her, and my stomach tensed up as I opened it. Tears started flowing as I read it. Not only did she rebuke my attempt at a peaceful reconciliation and refuse to accept my apology, but she spewed so much hatred toward me. To this day, I still have no idea why she despises me so much, but after years of mental torment from trying to figure it out, I finally found peace when I learned to accept what it was without ever knowing.

Life Lessons

- No matter what anybody thinks of you, God loves and values you just as He created you.
- The pain of being rejected or unloved by a parent whose role is to protect and love you unconditionally is like no other, and it affects the way we see and

respond to the world around us. But God adopts you as His own and can heal those deep-seeded wounds.

- Realize that our parents are only human and will never be perfect. They, too, are healing from their own past wounds and childhood traumas.
- You can stop the cycle of abuse by showing your own children the love and acceptance you so desperately needed and deserved.
- Healing comes when we choose to forgive the wrongdoings of our parents and understand that we, too, will sometimes need forgiveness from our own children.

Prayer: *I pray for anyone who has ever been rejected or abandoned by a parent or guardian would know the immense love that your heavenly Father has for you and that He will never leave you nor forsake you. Amen.*

Declaration: *If my father or my mother forsake me, then the Lord will take care of me (Psalm 27:10).*

CHAPTER 3

UNEQUALLY YOKED

"Christ loved the church and gave himself up for her" (Ephesians 5:25, NIV).

I started dating my high school sweetheart when I was fourteen years old. We had been friends for a couple of years before we officially became a couple. We fell very much in love, or as in love as teenagers could be. We were so happy the first couple of years, and he treated me like a princess. He would surprise me often with gifts and flowers and thought the world of me. We spent most of our time outside of school together, always laughing and singing every '90s country song that came on the radio. It was like one of those high school movies directed by John Hughes, just without a happy ending.

One day, out of the blue, I got a call from a previous boyfriend that I had not seen in a few years. I lied to my current boyfriend and told him I was going to have lunch with my grandma but went to see my ex instead. I was just curious and a little flattered he even wanted to hang out. I don't know if his intention was to get me in bed, but he did. I felt so horrible and guilty afterward that I told my boyfriend that night as I could not keep it a secret. It broke his heart, and nothing was ever the same again. By the way, my ex never contacted me again.

The next day, my boyfriend turned completely jealous and possessive. He started losing his temper quickly, violently and frequently. Shortly after this incident, we got into a heated argument about my ex while I was driving my mother's car. He got so upset that he pushed his feet on the front windshield and cracked it. This behavior became our new normal for the duration of our relationship, but I stayed because I loved him. The violence only escalated, and we fought more and more often. I don't even remember what we would fight about most of the time, but it seemed that everything set him off, like forgetting to tell his mom goodbye. He was verbally and physically abusive, calling me names, pushing me up against the wall and even slapping me across the face. One day, we were arguing over something when he grabbed my hand and put his cigarette out on it, which I still have the scar.

At one point, he had gotten into some trouble for breaking and entering and ended up serving three months in the county jail. I went to visit him every week. In the meantime, I rented an apartment above his aunt's house and made it a home for us when he got out. He apologized regularly while in jail and promised never to hit me again.

Of course, I believed him. Within a week of his release, he had already pinned me against the wall again. During another fight, he got on top of me and held me down on the bed. When I tried screaming for help, he shoved a sock in my mouth so nobody could hear me. I was able to break free and call the police for help. He got arrested, and his stepdad blamed me for getting him in trouble when he saw me at the police station.

Another time, while I was bathing in one of those cast iron bathtubs, he got so mad that he was able to pick up one end of the tub while it was full of water and me in it. A bunch of the water spilled over and leaked through to his aunt's walls and floors, and she had to have the carpet replaced. She was so upset she yelled at me. The whole time, my boyfriend stood behind her, silently laughing at me for getting the blame. This was my life, and I didn't know how to get out. I loved him and didn't think I could live without him.

In fact, I was so obsessed with being with him that I harmed myself on a couple of occasions because I couldn't be with him. A few years earlier, my mom grounded me, and I was so upset that I tried overdosing on twenty-four aspirin. Luckily, I just ended up vomiting all night. Another time, my boyfriend was going out with his friends, and I couldn't go, so I lost all control and stabbed myself in the head several times with a pair of scissors. Thankfully, I didn't go deep enough to bleed, but I had welts for a while. During my senior year of high school, I dropped out so that I could be with him every day since he had already dropped out.

There were many times that different people tried rescuing me or that I wanted to leave him, but I was too attached. We did break up for a while when I stayed with a relative out of town and got my GED, but I found my way back to him. Things were bliss for a short time, and I ended up getting pregnant. I was eighteen years old and scared and excited at the same time. Because we lived in a Christian community, I was worried that we would not be able to find an apartment while having a child out of wedlock, so I insisted we get married. One month before our baby arrived, my dad walked me down the aisle.

We were definitely not the definition of what a marriage should be. He slept on the couch, and I slept in the bed with our newborn baby. He would go out with his friends while my family watched our daughter so I could go to work. He couldn't hold a steady job. He would lie around watching television while I took our daughter and dirty clothes to the laundromat. Occasionally, he would help carry a basket up our long set of stairs. However, if he got mad at me, he would take all the folded laundry and throw them around the living room. I grew to utterly despise him and constantly looked for a way out for me and our daughter. I was so codependent that I felt I could not leave him without having somebody else to depend on. I could not imagine being alone.

Eventually, it happened. I packed up my stuff for the last time and left. I had a new hope on the horizon. Of course, my husband did not like the idea of my new plan without him and was not going to easily let me go. He caused a lot of drama by involving our families or the police with lies and manipulation. A few times, he waited for me as I was driving home from work and would chase me off the road, even though our daughter was in the vehicle. Eventually, he realized I was not coming back, and we got divorced.

I immediately started dating a new man and believed he was my knight in shining armor. I thought I could finally have the fairytale that I always wanted. He was so handsome, responsible and actually had a job with a skilled trade. I thought my dreams were finally coming true. Of course, we had a lot of details to sort out with our new life together. After a few short months of dating, I found myself homeless and showed up on his doorstep with a laundry basket on one hip and a baby on the other. We were both going through ugly divorces at the time, so we decided to lean on each other.

From there, we started blending our families together. He had three small children, and I had my little girl. We were both still raw from going through our divorces, so neither one of us had the desire to remarry again. It definitely wasn't picture-perfect, and we had a lot of uproar from both sides of our families. Plus, we were both going through our own custody battles with our exes and working on dividing up assets and debts, which were more debts than assets. Early on, he showed signs of jealousy and control, but I just felt so privileged that he even wanted to be with me that I ignored it. Some of my friends and family were immediately concerned with how he treated me, but I had no idea what they were talking about. I felt that as long as we had each other, we would be fine. He desired me, and I desired to be desired. I thought he hung the moon, and I would do anything to keep him happy so that he would keep me.

I was too infatuated to realize that his anger was quickly teaching me what he liked and didn't like. If he didn't agree with something I did or said, he would get quite upset with me, so I tried really hard not to do anything wrong. He was six years older than me and pretty set in his ways. He believed in the old-fashioned role of a man and a woman, meaning the man went to work and the woman cooked, cleaned, took care of the children and served the man. However, being a modern woman, I could work full-time to help out with the finances as well. In the beginning, I kept up with all of his demands. I was young, full of energy and eager to prove my worthiness. I was responsible, worked hard and had excellent credit. If we needed anything that we couldn't afford with cash, I had plenty of credit cards available. But when the monthly bills arrived, he would get upset that I wanted to make at least the minimum payments on them. It was not long until I had a mound of debt that I could not afford to keep up with. But he was happy, so I was happy because he was happy. And things always worked out better for us when he was happy.

At first, I did not know how to cook very well, especially the meat and potatoes kind of meals he requested, but I learned the best I could. He worked long hours standing on his feet, so I didn't hesitate to sit on the floor and massage them every night. Once we got into our rhythm, we didn't fight much, and I felt pretty safe. It was a lot better than being pushed around or called horrible names. In fact, it took me about a year to stop flinching whenever he would lift his arms to give me a hug because I was expecting to get hit. It wasn't until a couple of years later that I came home a little late, and it made him go into a fit of rage to the point he pinned me against the wall with his hand around my throat. Thankfully, that was the one and only time he ever got physically violent with me.

After a few years together, I realized that I never wanted to live without him, so we decided to make it official. We got married on Valentine's Day in the courthouse with just our closest family and friends. He surprised me with a night away after our ceremony to a quaint, secluded cabin a couple of hours north. It was so romantic and beautiful. I was so excited to celebrate our relationship and loved having a husband with whom I could spend the rest of my life. He was committed and faithful, and I couldn't have been happier. I was ready to continue building a life together for us and our children. We were finally a real family.

Even though he was not a Christian, nor wanted anything to do with the faith I believed in, he did not hinder me from going to church or taking the children. Our kids ranged from one to six years old when we first started dating, so I was able to lead them to the Lord while they were still young. Over time, all four of our children accepted Christ as their Savior, and the kids and I got baptized together. I prayed for my husband's heart to change for several years and continued to show him the love and devotion of a submissive wife. I was careful to avoid putting pressure on him to come with us to church, but I would occasionally ask him as a reminder that he was always invited.

Eventually, God created an opportunity for him to work with a Christian-owned company, so he had some mentorship there. One night, about ten years into our marriage, he finally asked me to lead him in prayer to accept Jesus Christ as his Savior. Another long-awaited answer to my prayers. I believed God had finally changed his heart and that we could finally be the happily married couple I had always prayed for since the very beginning of our relationship.

One evening, as I was working on this book, I believe God showed me that a relationship needs to have the following essential elements in order to have a life-long, fulfilling marriage. I call these the seven Cs of marriage, and I am not talking about the same seven seas that Annie Lennox sings about. After putting this together, I also realized that it would be very difficult to achieve a successful marriage with any one of these components missing. It may not be impossible to sustain, but it probably won't be very satisfying for its duration. Let's take a look.

Chemistry—This is that initial attraction or spark that you cannot quite explain. You either have it or you don't, and you probably won't even make it past hello without this. My problem was that it only took chemistry for me to jump in feet first, not realizing that it takes a lot more than this to make it the long haul.

Compatibility—Once you know that you have a mutual connection, compatibility is quite important. And not necessarily regarding interests and hobbies but, more importantly, beliefs, values and future goals. If one wants a house full of children and the other one has no desire for kids, or one has visions of settling down on a farm and the other wants to be a missionary in other countries, you might want to rethink building a lifelong commitment together.

Compromise—This attribute helps in the areas where two people are not completely compatible. If one likes comedies and the other likes action movies, then date nights should include taking turns enjoying each other's preferences. Or holidays are equally shared between both sides of your families. The ability to compromise is so important because this should be an equal partnership and not about meeting the wants and needs of just one person. However, this does not mean compromising your core values and beliefs; this should be covered already in the compatibility section.

Communication—Fully understand that men and women seem to speak entirely different languages at times, but communication does not have to be that difficult. A healthy relationship would give both partners a safe place to express their needs, wants and concerns without the fear of punishment, abuse or retribution. In neglecting the importance of healthy conversation, any relationship is in danger of eventually breaking down.

Compassion—This is where your genuine feelings for your partner are revealed. Compassion includes the emotional support, care and value you place on your spouse. If your heart is hardened toward each other, the whole structure of your relationship will be negatively affected.

Commitment—If you want to enjoy the benefits of a long-term relationship, such as marriage, you obviously need to be willing and ready to commit. There is no way around this one. When you find the right person that you want to spend the rest of your life with, you are choosing to commit yourself, your time, your finances and your future decisions together. This is where two become one, and you both decide to take on life together.

Christ—I saved the most important for last. Without Christ, we would barely be able to give even the slightest amount of ourselves needed to sustain such a lifelong covenant. Our relationship with Christ helps give us the strength, humility and desire to accomplish all of the above. He created, defined and showed us, by example, what the ultimate marriage looks like as He laid down His life for His bride.

Life Lessons

- Marriage was created by God to be the most beautiful and intimate human relationship between one man and one woman as a lifelong covenant.

- God's Word says that we are to submit to one another, as the wife respects her husband and the husband loves his wife just as Christ loved His church.

- Love and respect are both equally honorable because love is respectful, and respect is an act of love.

- Marriage is a partnership between two individuals, each having their own gifts, skills, passions, and roles. Yet, each person is considered equal, neither being more valuable than the other.

- A marital relationship is more likely to be fruitful when encouraged and supported by community and loved ones. Never be too afraid or ashamed to ask for counsel or help, regardless of how long or recently you have been married. We are always learning, growing and healing. So, choose to create the safe, supportive and intimate relationship that God has intended for both of you.

- Abuse is not love, and love is not abusive. Abuse should never be accepted or tolerated in any relationship. Please seek professional advice if you think you are in an abusive relationship.

Prayer: *I pray for every marriage to be a mere reflection of what Jesus Christ displayed with His great love for His bride, the church, by giving up Himself as an ultimate sacrifice. Amen.*

Declaration: *God rejoices over me as a bridegroom rejoices over his bride (Isaiah 62:5).*

CHAPTER 4

ADDICTED

"For your love is better than wine"
(Song of Solomon 1:2, ESV).

An addiction is basically any potentially harmful activity, substance or thing that we have become so dependent on that we believe we have to have it in order to find enjoyment or fulfillment in our lives. It is a habit or state of mind in which we have allowed something to gain power and control over us and has become a priority in our lives. The degree of how much an addiction affects somebody can vary greatly from person to person. Some lose everything to keep their addiction: their loved ones, their home, their job, and even their life. But it usually starts the same way for each of us. We begin with trying to find a quick fix or a way to detach from the stress and worries of the world, but eventually, your flesh grows more and more dependent on this thing to maintain some level of comfort and momentary satisfaction as it did in the beginning. This is the vicious cycle that we get trapped in, and unfortunately, there is always a low after each high. While some people may be able to enjoy certain things in moderation, others may struggle to maintain balance or control, and their addiction can quickly spiral out of control.

Addictions come in many forms, and honestly, almost anything can become an addiction. Drugs, alcohol, cigarettes, gambling and pornography are all too common. But what about food, social media or some of our relationships? Even well-intentioned objectives can easily become excessive when not kept in proper balance, such as diet, exercise or religious activities. Or maybe you had an injury at no fault of your own that required a prescription drug that inadvertently caused you to become physically dependent. In fact, opioid use is now at epidemic levels and is just as commonly misused as illegal street drugs. Regardless of the preferred substance or object of a person's addiction, although some are much more dangerous than others, they basically all have the same root cause. It is a need or desire to mask, hide or relieve the pain that is hurting us. We hate pain! Whether it's emotional pain like shame, loneliness, hopelessness or physical pain, we will go to great lengths to avoid or run from it.

I was raised by and around recovering addicts my entire childhood. When I was born, my dad was a heavy drug user and dealer. Thankfully, while I was still quite young and as far back as I can remember, my dad had gone through recovery and got sober. My brother and I were dragged to N. A. (Narcotics Anonymous) meetings several times a week for years. Eventually, he met his second wife there. My mom had struggled with codependency issues, so she went to Al-anon, which was a group intended for spouses of alcoholics. Then, my stepdad was in A. A. (Alcoholics Anonymous). As I got older, I attended Alateen, which was for the children of alcoholics. All of these people were a big part of our lives well into my teenage years. We hung out together, went on camping trips, dances and even church. I am still close friends with many of the kids I grew up with in these recovery groups.

I learned a lot of valuable things growing up in that environment. Such as memorizing the Lord's Prayer, the Serenity Prayer and relying on a higher power for our strength and sanity. I found that there are a lot of people struggling with addictions, that they can lean on each other and not battle it alone. Another important realization was that everybody was having a good time while being sober, and they didn't need drugs or alcohol to have fun. And I learned that recovering addicts love coffee, lots of coffee! I guess we all need something to get by.

I'm not sure if most people or just certain personality types, like mine, struggle more with having what's commonly referred to as an addictive personality. I used to believe that, but now I think we use that phrase much more as an excuse by thinking that our nature is more suscepti-ble to becoming an addict than the average person. When in reality, every one of us has weaknesses to temptation just as much as the next person. Even the Bible says in 1 Corinthians 10:13 that the temptations in our life are no different from what others experience. I am naturally an all-or-nothing thinker, so it can be a struggle to keep bal-ance in many areas of my life. This kind of logic keeps me bouncing from one extreme to another. For example, going from dieting to binging, excessive worrying to not caring at all or working hard to achieve my goals but then giving up somewhere along the way. My mind sees this great big world and all its possibilities, but when it gets too hard, I shut everything down and hide. I tend to go from being a social butterfly and interacting with so many people, but as soon as I get hurt by someone, I retreat back into the safety of isolation. These perfectionistic expectations can be a breeding ground for addiction because of the constant battle to be perfect or do everything perfectly and then consider it a failure every time you fall short.

I have had to overcome many different addictions over the past forty years and still continue to fight for my own recovery. My first addiction came when I fell in love with food as a young girl; pasta, cereal and chocolate were some of my favorites. I am definitely a carby! Decades later, I still find myself eating so fast that I don't even remember taking the first bite because I was too focused on taking the next one. I had made food one of my best friends. Food became my crutch whether I was celebrating, mourning or just plain bored.

Then, I had my first cigarette at thirteen years old, and it did not take long to get hooked. It wasn't long before I was doing whatever I had to get my next one. I would smoke the half-cigarette butts I found in my parents' ashtrays, take some from their packs laying around the house or go to the local bowling alley, where they still had an unattended cigarette machine. I even put a hole in the screen of my bedroom window so that the neighborhood boys could give me one when they came to hang out in the middle of the night. I didn't want my parents to know I was smoking, so I would hide in my closet and smoke my cigarettes. But then all of my clothes reeked of smoke. I was already living the life of an addict. We do whatever it takes to get our next fix and try to hide the truth of what we are doing from almost everyone around us.

I had never drunk alcohol or gotten drunk for the first time until my twenty-first birthday on an entire bottle of Boone's Farm, and all I remember is the whole world was spinning. I had tried marijuana a couple of times as a teenager and got so high that my heart felt like it was going to beat out of my chest, and I literally thought I was going to die. By the grace of God, I was never exposed or tempted to try any hard drugs before. But going into my twenties, life got absolutely crazy. I was going through a nasty divorce and custody battle, and I had started dating someone who was going through the same thing with his three small children. My family was in an uproar over my situation; my stepmom despised me, and I was basically homeless with a baby. There was so much chaos and drama at that time, and I was so angry at the world. I just wanted peace or to escape, but there was nowhere to go.

I didn't like the effects of alcohol or that you can't function well while drunk, and I didn't want to deal with hangovers. I had two bad experiences with smoking marijuana in the past, so I was hesitant to try it again but still a little curious. Shortly after we started dating, I found out that my new boyfriend smoked marijuana often. He didn't want to influence me into it, so one evening, when he was about to take a shower, he left a joint on the table and said I could do what I wanted with it. I decided to light it up and see how it would affect me this time. I must have really enjoyed it because it became my new best friend. When I was high, I didn't have a care in the world, and I laughed at every stupid thought in my head or whatever somebody else would say. And when I wasn't high, I was so mad and bitter that I could feel all the chaos within and around me. At first, I started out just smoking marijuana on the weekends. Of course, as my tolerance level grew, I started smoking more and more often. Before I knew it, I was high every night and then all day, every day. Life was much better when I was high, so I wanted to be high all the time! I didn't care how we got it, where we got it from or how much it cost. Once, I even made him go out in a blizzard, where he could not see two feet in front of him, just to get me another joint.

When people say you cannot become addicted to marijuana, well, I did. In fact, just try to take it away from someone who smokes regularly and see how they will react...just like an addict. Although you may not have the same physical withdrawals as many other drugs, there is still an emotional and psychological dependency to regular usage. Eventually, our usage capped out to where we were smoking about an ounce a week together, which cost around $120 back then. We would be considered functioning addicts, and there are many of them out here. You may know one or be one yourself. They are people who can go to work every day, be responsible for paying their bills and take care of their families' needs, all while living a lifestyle of being high or intoxicated on a regular basis. This was our routine for five years. After a couple of years, though, I didn't want to be high anymore, but I could no longer cope with the demands of life and the pain of my past without it.

The one good thing through all of this was that even with the shame of trying to hide my addiction from people, it never caused me to try to hide from God or doubt His existence. Even with all of my issues, drug use and living a sinful lifestyle, I still believed in God and that He still cared. So, when I came to the point in my life where I wanted to come back to the Lord, I did not hesitate. I couldn't get sober on my own, but I knew I needed God. I decided it was better to come to Him high than not at all, so I would puff my pipe while reading my Bible or even before church.

Now, before you judge me for my behavior while in the presence of God, may we be reminded that we are always in the presence of God, and there is nothing that He doesn't see. The good news for us is that Christ died for us while we were yet sinners, according to Romans 5:8. I love in Mark 2:16–17 when the Pharisees asked why Jesus was eating with the sinners, He replied that it is the sick that need a doctor, not the healthy and that He came for those who know they sin, not those who think they are righteous. Therefore, we can come boldly to the throne of grace as it says in Hebrews 4:16. And we must continually remind ourselves that we desperately need God's grace just as much on our good days as we do on our bad days.

If we can be removed from church for our sins, then the doors would be completely closed to each one of us. God wants us to show up with an open and honest heart that seeks to know Him more. Jesus did not come so we could have a religion but rather a relationship with our Heavenly Father. Please let me take a moment to sincerely apologize, as a believer and follower of Jesus Christ, if you have ever been told or made to feel that you are not good enough to enter the presence of God because no one, not even one, is righteous in their own effort. Religion does not save us any more than it did with the Pharisees. Only Jesus has the power to save us, heal us and set us free. And we cannot receive our healing until we first come to the Healer, not the other way around.

God knew the desire of my heart and that I really wanted to be free, but He also knew I felt stuck in my addiction. A few years after I started working on my relationship with the Lord, my (now) husband and I had a trip planned to Florida. Two weeks before our vacation, the Holy Spirit must have given me an awareness that He was about to do something big, and I felt that it was in regard to my dependency on marijuana. Since we were going to fly, I knew that we would not be able to bring any with us, so I accepted the fact that I would have to go an entire week without getting high.

Well, come to find out, God did have a plan; I just didn't know it would be so painful. The night before our flight, we were busy packing and, of course, getting high. I was so excited about the trip that I took a long drag from the pipe, ran across the house to my husband, and I was going to blow it into his mouth (I know it sounds silly, but it's called shotgunning). However, by the time I got to him, I blacked out from holding it in too long and fell to the ground. He caught me when I was halfway to the floor, but we heard a loud crack. When I stood up, he let me go, and I fell again. After a trip to the emergency room, they found that I had broken my foot in two spots and gave me Vicodin for the pain. We still made our flight the next morning, but I couldn't do much of anything other than float around the pool at our rental house the entire stay. This was not the plan I had in mind, but I guess God knows what's best.

At the end of the week, we safely flew back to the Chicago airport, where a friend and his girlfriend picked us up to drive us back home. They were close friends of ours that we got high with often, so it was not a surprise when he pulled out a joint before we even got out of the airport parking lot. We lit it up, and I took a few puffs just like I had so many times before, but this time, the effect was completely different. I literally thought I was going to die.

I was so scared; my heart was racing, and my brain felt like it was comatose. I thought we were going to have to stop at a hospital, but I just laid in the back seat the entire two-and-a-half-hour ride home, trying to remain calm. At that point, I knew I was never going to smoke marijuana again. As soon as we pulled into our driveway, I became completely sober, and all the effects wore off. I never had a single puff since that moment. God really did have a plan to set me free. To this day, I still don't know what caused me to have such a severe reaction, but I don't care. I am just so grateful to be free and that I never touched it again.

Are you struggling with an addiction? If so, God truly wants to set you free, too. Hopefully, you won't have to break any bones like me. If you're not sure, here are a few questions you can ask yourself. If you cannot answer honestly or are not sure, maybe a close friend or relative can help you see from a clearer perspective. Sometimes, the people around us can see us better than we can see ourselves, regardless of how hard we try to hide it.

- Do you need this thing regularly to make you feel happy or escape reality?
- What or who are you willing to sacrifice to get it?
- How would you react if this item was removed from your life?
- Would you feel depressed, anxious or lost if you nev-

er had this thing again?

If you said yes to any of these questions, you may be struggling with an addiction. First of all, I want to commend you for being honest with yourself or another person. The first step to recovery is admitting that we have a problem. Now, please do not beat yourself up on how you got into this situation or because you haven't been strong enough to get out. In 1 Corinthians 10:13, we are told that there is no temptation that has overtaken us that is not common to man, but God is faithful in making a way out. Next, find a trusted friend or counselor with whom you can talk about what you are going through so that you don't have to face this alone. Finally, do whatever you need to find freedom. Whether that is joining a small group, therapy, recovery program, or rehabilitation center. Just do not be afraid to ask for help. Your life is worth fighting for, and trust that God is fighting for you, too.

Life Lessons

- Please know that you are not alone when it comes to dealing with addiction, for we all do, whether we admit it or not.

- It is best not to try to overcome an addiction by yourself. The odds of success and recovery greatly increase when you have support and accountability.

- Do not let the guilt and shame from your addiction keep you from asking for help because God designed us to hold one another up in times of trouble.
- Remember, addiction is our way of relieving or escaping the discomfort of pain, but the only true way to be free is to face it so that you can heal from it.
- Instead of letting your shortcomings and weaknesses hinder your relationship with God, let them be the reason you draw closer to Him for the strength and comfort you need.

Prayer: *Lord, I pray that anyone struggling with any addictions would be led to Your path of freedom, right now, in the mighty name of Jesus. Amen.*

Declaration: *I call upon the Lord, and He answers me; He sets me free (Psalm 118:5).*

CHAPTER 5

LURES OF LUST

"My beloved is mine and I am his"
(Song of Solomon 2:16, NIV).

My generation was born near the end of the sexual revolution that exploded here in the United States between the 1960s and 1970s. That could even be why many of us are here today. It was a time when sex, drugs and rock n' roll took over television, homes and, eventually, the world. What started out as a seductive pelvic roll from Elvis in 1954 led us to Madonna rolling around on stage in her lingerie, singing "Like a Virgin" thirty years later.

Now, almost another forty years, and music artists are barely wearing anything. They look more like they belong in the adult film industry than in music videos. We can only imagine how much further this will go. In fact, within the past few years of writing this chapter, we now have children confused about what gender they are. With the combination of the hippies' free love movement and women's liberation sending us on a momentum that has no intention of stopping, we came into the era of "lay down, I think I love you." I stole that line from my hippie aunt.

As a woman, I have to say that some good has come to us as women in that we have gained the right to equality and a voice to be heard. Now, I do believe that the Word of God created an order of authority for man to be the head of the household and lead his family, but we have to remember this was ordained by God as a position of honor and responsibility and not because men did anything to deserve it. Therefore, we have seen this power of authority abused for many generations, leading to the revolt of oppressed women. However, even I can admit that maybe we pushed back a little too far and opened Pandora's box, which will probably never be closed again. Yet, I do not believe that all hope is lost.

Growing up in a highly sexualized environment, from movies, music and my own childhood sexual abuse, the only form of love I could relate to was through physical intimacy. In fact, I was just thirteen years old when I became sexually active. I was timid and had very low self-esteem and a desperate need to be loved, so it didn't take much effort for a boy to get my attention. I was too shy to speak up and would do almost anything they wanted to keep them coming back. I've always been attracted to the bad boys, and for some reason, they were attracted to me. It must have been something about their outspoken nature, rebellious attitude or smooth-talking charm that would draw me in. To this day, I still have a desire to capture their hearts and try to change or rescue them, even though that has never worked for me.

In the summer of 1991, I spent many nights sneaking out with a boy who had a reputation for being with a lot of girls. Usually, I would crawl out my window, and we would end up in somebody's basement, a stranger's boat or just running around the streets. It didn't matter as long as I made it back to my bedroom before the morning when my mom came home from working the third shift. One night, while we were walking around the neighborhood, a police officer saw us and started to chase after us. We ran so fast in between the houses and down the alleys until we safely ended up back at my house. Another time, I snuck out by myself, and a cop started chasing after me. I hid in some bushes and tried not to even breathe until I could no longer hear him walking around. Somehow, I made it back home again without getting caught. Eventually, I realized that it would just be better to wait to come home until after the sun came up when curfew restrictions were lifted (you know, rather than just not sneak out at all).

Once, when my boyfriend jumped out of my window, his foot got caught in my blinds and caused a loud crashing sound outside of my bedroom. When my stepdad went to check out the noise and saw my screen lying on the ground, he nailed it shut the very next morning. In which, I then proceeded to go out the front door or window. Or the time my best friend and I pushed another one of my boyfriend's Trans Am down her driveway and started it in the street so that we didn't wake her parents up. We even put pillows and stuffed animals under our blankets to make it look like we were sleeping, but instead, we met up with completely unknown guys down by the river. Another time, my friends and I got a ride home from the park with some gang members. I could go on and on with story after story, but I think you get the point. It was only by God's grace and protection that I made it home safe all those years or that nothing horrible happened to me because many girls have not been so lucky.

Later in my teenage years, I started having an attraction to women. I sometimes wondered if it was because of all the abuse from men in my life that could have triggered me to have such a strong desire to be with a woman. Don't get me wrong, I was still very much interested in men, but something was even more luring to me about women. I had done some experimenting with a girlfriend of mine when I was younger, but it wasn't until my early twenties that I had my first same-sex experience. I had recently married my second husband, and he knew of my interest in women. Honestly, it was probably one of the things that attracted him to me. One evening, while hanging out with friends and family at a campground, I unexpectedly met a woman who seemed to be attracted to me. We had all been drinking, and one thing led to another. After that night, she became a third partner in our relationship. Now, before your mouth drops, let me just say that I am not the first woman to think it was a good idea to bring another woman into a marriage. I am reminded that it was Sarah's idea to have her husband, Abraham, lay with her maidservant to conceive a son. Obviously, we don't always think the whole thing through before getting ourselves into trouble. In fact, we are still dealing with the consequences of that decision with the continued conflict between Israel and Palestine today, but that's another story.

Anyway, it was like a fantasy come true where I could have the best of both worlds, enjoying the strength and masculinity of a man and the soft, feminine touch of a woman. However, reality never turns out the same as our fantasies. It wasn't long until I felt like the third wheel in my own marriage and extreme jealousy because my husband seemed to desire this other woman more than he did me. Again, Sarah ended up feeling the same way towards Hagar, even though it was our own harebrained idea. Eventually, I could not handle all the emotions and strain this was causing in my relationship with my husband, and I just wanted him back to myself. Also, friends and family started to find out about our secret lifestyle, and that caused a whole bunch of backlash. I decided that I just wanted normalcy and peace back with myself and everyone around me. I had quickly fallen into a very perverse and lustful stupor, but it didn't take long for the consequences of reality to wake me back up.

At this point, I hadn't even put God into the equation or considered what He wanted for my life. I just felt the painful consequences of my unwise actions and changed course. You never really know how strong the desires of your flesh are until you come face to face with your weaknesses. So, we closed that door and concentrated on our marriage and our newly blended family. For many years, we stayed committed to building our life together. I sought my relationship with God again and started bringing our children to church. I didn't struggle anymore with the desire to be with a woman and believed that God had actually changed the desires of my heart.

Over a decade later and years into my healing journey from much of my childhood abuse, I had become stronger in my faith and more dedicated to my family, my husband and God than ever before. I accepted a job offer with a reputable Christian organization, and even though it was not a prestigious position by any means, I was happy and content that God was providing what we needed. I was working among mostly Christian-professing women, yet I found it hard to find acceptance with them. I didn't seem to fit in and thought maybe I was too joyous or appeared holier than thou since I had recently been in one of those very spirit-filled seasons of my life.

A few weeks into my new job, one of the girls who had been training me jokingly shouted to the other women that she was going to corrupt me as we headed off to our jobs. I instantly replied with such confidence that I was incorruptible. Well, it wasn't long before I would eat those words and be reminded that pride cometh before the fall. Although I did not see it at the time as prideful, I just thought I was being a devout, obedient woman of God. I can't help but think of Peter when Jesus told him that He would pray for him just before going to the cross. Peter, so assured of his faithfulness to Christ, replied that he didn't need prayer because he was willing to follow Jesus to prison or even unto death. Jesus just looks at Peter with sorrow, already knowing his weakness, and tells him how he will deny Him three times before the rooster crows.

Well, I found that life reveals two things: how strong we are and how weak we are. It wasn't long after my firm belief of being incorruptible that I developed a physically intimate relationship with that woman. I fell fast, I fell hard, and I may have even fallen in love. Of course, I was still married, so my husband was also involved. Here I am, thousands of generations later, and still following in the footsteps of our first mother, Eve. Now, unlike Sarah, Eve did not bring her husband another woman, but she did convince him to partake in eating the forbidden fruit. For the sins of the world have been the same since the very beginning: the lust of the flesh, the lust of the eyes and the pride of life, as written in 1 John 2:16.

Part of me knew beforehand how this was going to end, just like it had previously, but the desire was too strong for me to withstand. It wasn't long before I started feeling like a third wheel again, and my husband had more desire to be with her than with me. And, honestly, I probably had more desire to be with her than with him. From the beginning of my relationship with my husband, I had so badly wanted the love and affection from him that he couldn't seem to give. I prayed for him to care about me and our children like we really meant something to him. I patiently waited for many years but still had not seen my prayers answered. I finally came to the point where I accepted the fact that he was just not capable until I saw him treat her and her children the way I had hoped and dreamed he would treat us. I was so devastated and heartbroken. Our children were older at this time, so our lifestyle choices were no secret, which caused a lot of family uproar again. Eventually, I ended the relationship. I hurt her, I hurt my family, I hurt my marriage and I surely hurt God.

I always loved God, but obviously not enough to obey Him. I wanted to believe that I was covered by grace and forgiveness so I could ignore the warnings that Paul gives to Christians about living a sinful lifestyle. I was constantly wrestling with the thoughts of salvation being based on faith, not works. So, if we cannot earn it, can we lose it? Could I live any way I wanted and still be a Christian? Are our sins truly covered by the cross, or are there contingencies based on our behaviors? I know these are all commonly asked questions by believers and have been extensively debated since the beginning of the early church.

Well, I will never forget the vision that God gave me during this season of my life. We were all asleep when I was abruptly awakened in the middle of the night. I looked up to the ceiling, and what appeared to be the sky opened above me. The clouds parted, and I saw Jesus come back for His people. It was the most vivid, surreal vision I had ever seen at this point in my life. It felt so real! It happened so fast, like a thief in the night, just as the Bible warns. Before I could blink my eyes, the sky closed up, and He was gone…but I was left behind. It was the most frightening and horrifying feeling of regret that I will forever remember. My heart sank with such agony as I was pleading for a second chance. I was begging God to come back and crying for Him not to leave me. I am so thankful to God for His mercy and that He chose to let me know what could happen and gave me a chance to change my life. This time was a warning, but one day, it will be too late. I can promise that it will be something that none of us will ever want to experience.

By now, we can see how much sexual immorality has greatly and negatively impacted my life and so many around me, whether it was by my own sin or the sins of others. The Bible says that every sin is outside the body, except sexual sin, which is against your own body. We see the prevalence of sexual sin vastly throughout the whole world now. We have become our own gods and been deceived into believing that we can do whatever we want with our bodies without consequence. God created sex. Therefore, He thinks it is good and beautiful, but only within His terms and conditions and for good reason. We made it all about our own perverted pleasures, and now we see the state of chaos and confusion we are in with gender identity issues, prostitution, fornication, adultery, homosexuality, rape and incest.

Sex was never meant to just be casual. First Corinthians 6:16 says that even if a man sleeps with a prostitute, they become one. This means that for those of us living in this generation, many have been bonded to several different people they do not even know of; not only that, but sexually transmitted infections are sky-high. And almost half of all pregnancies are unplanned or unwanted, resulting in a significant rise in abortions. In fact, statistics show that one in three women will terminate an unplanned pregnancy at least once in her lifetime. It is recorded that 73 million babies are aborted every year, that is approximately 200,000 per day. This is the very sad and real condition our world is in right now.

With all of my reckless and careless decisions, I was grateful for all of the years that I did not end up in this situation…until I did. I found myself in another extremely abusive relationship, one that God had even warned me to stay away from in a dream, but I didn't listen. Then, I became so enmeshed with him emotionally and physically that it took several attempts to end it over a two-year period. I thought, or hoped, as I had many times before, that I was finally strong enough to detach and move on to the next level of my healing when I found out I was pregnant. I was devastated and scared due to the abuse in the relationship, my age, my weight, my mental health and my finances. Everything about this situation was high risk. I felt stuck thinking that I could not do this on my own and

I definitely could not safely raise a child with him. After several weeks of crying and agonizing over every possible option and outcome, I chose to terminate the pregnancy.

This is a situation and decision no woman ever wants to be in. We shouldn't even be the ones to play God and determine whether to give or take life away. Abortion equals death, plain and simple. And because this goes against all that is natural, maternal and moral, the mother will grieve the loss of their child for the rest of their life, even though she was the one who made that decision. She will mourn not ever being able to hold or nurture her baby and see the life that would have been. She may also struggle with the guilt and shame that abortion causes until she receives the healing work that only God can provide, which He can and will do when we turn to Him.

Regardless of opinion or what one may have been told, I firmly believe that life starts at conception. In fact, the entire DNA of a person is instantly created when the sperm fertilizes the egg. And a fetus has a heartbeat as early as eighteen days after conception, well before most women even find out they are pregnant. The baby's limbs, fingers and toes grow rapidly, as well as their brain and organs start to develop. Their genetic features are already determined, such as gender, hair and eye color. King David writes in the Psalms how God wove his innermost being in his mother's womb and confirms that is when life starts to take form. While we're speaking of David, let us look further into his life and see how the consequences of his sins affected him and those around him.

He was anointed to become the king of Israel, even while he was still a shepherd boy and God used him to do amazing things. He killed the Philistine giant, Goliath, with just a sling and stone and killed a lion and a bear with his own hands. He was considered a man after God's own heart and was very faithful to God. It was only after he became king and saw so many glorious works that the Lord had done for and through him that his lustful desires eventually overtook him when he saw the beautiful Bathsheba bathing on a roof. She was married, in fact, to one of David's most loyal soldiers who was serving in battle at the time. David gave the order to bring Bathsheba to him, which doesn't really sound like much of a choice to her, but he laid with her, and she became pregnant. To cover up the sin of their affair, David sent for her husband, hoping he would sleep with his wife and assume the baby was his. But, when that plan did not work, he had her husband sent back out to the front lines of the war, surely to be killed in battle. Another ploy to conceal what he had done. He then marries Bathsheba, who is now grieving the loss of her first husband. When the baby is born, God is so displeased with all of David's actions that He sends a prophet to reveal exactly the nature of what he had done. David wept and repented. But the consequence of his sins was that the baby got sick, and even though David prayed and fasted for God to save his child, the baby died. David, in his mourning, still chose to get up and worship God.

Fortunately, the story doesn't end here because we have a God that redeems and restores. Amidst David's worship, he claimed that even though his baby would not return to him here on Earth, he would someday be reunited with him in heaven. David was assured in his faith that his baby was safe with God and that he would see him again. What a promise we have that we can be reunited with our babies awaiting us in heaven, regardless if the loss was an act of our will or God's. He even went on to bless David and Bathsheba with another son named Solomon, who became the wisest man to ever live on the earth and wrote a majority of the Proverbs.

God has a redemptive plan for us, too, regardless of what we may have ever done. If we repent, turn from our evil ways, and seek a relationship with God, He is always willing and ready to forgive and heal us from our past mistakes. Even better than that, He wants to give us an even better future. Jesus says in John 10:10 that the thief only comes to steal, kill and destroy but that He came to give us an abundant life. Not just enough, not barely getting by, but a life filled with peace, joy and prosperity. Life and death are set before us; let's choose life.

Life Lessons

- God created sex to be the most sacred form of intimacy between a man and woman within the covenant of marriage, and His design never changed, even if the world's has.

- If you struggle with any type of sexual immorality and want help, find a trusted friend or counselor and lean on God to show you the way out. It's not too late to repent and change directions.

- If you are facing an unplanned pregnancy, know that you are not alone. There is support to help you through all of your options before making a life-changing decision.

- If you or someone you know is struggling with the grief of having an abortion, whether recently or many years ago, please seek professional counseling or a post-abortive ministry to help you heal and be set free from the guilt and shame.

Prayer: *Lord, I pray that we would choose to use our bodies to glorify You and that You would deliver us from any temptation. Amen.*

Declaration: *My body is the temple of the Holy Spirit, and I have been bought at a high price (1 Corinthians 6:19–20).*

CHAPTER 6

PARENT OR STEP-PARENT–SAME DIFFERENCE

"And I will be your Father, and you will be my sons and daughters" (2 Corinthians 6:18, NLT).

I was nineteen years old when I gave birth to a precious baby girl. The instant connection with her was overwhelmingly powerful without any attempt of my own doing. She was mine, and I absolutely loved her as a mother would love her child. I would give up my life for her without a doubt. In fact, having her actually saved my life many times and in many ways, just as I am sure many parents can say about their own children. By the time she was a toddler, I had to choose whether to give that same kind of love to three other children I did not give birth to.

I was twenty-one when I fell in love with a man who had three young children of his own. I immediately knew if we were going to make our relationship work, we had to be united in all ways, especially with our children. I never had the thought that this one was mine or these ones were his; we were just one family from the beginning. Of course, none of this happened overnight and took time. We were fortunate that our children were very young, so they could all adapt to this new family structure while in their earlier years. However, they were still very much impacted by the separation of their parents and had a lot of heartache and adjusting to do themselves. I couldn't just jump in and say, "Hi, I'm your new mom. How about a big family hug?"

Becoming a blended family is even harder than just becoming newlyweds. Instead of only two people starting a new life together, you now have multiple people with different personalities, perspectives and temperaments. But I can tell you that it is possible and absolutely worth it if you take the time and patience needed to grow together. Now, not only are the step-parents and children learning how to trust and support each other, but many other relationships that are involved. You have to adjust to your ex's and their ex's parenting schedules and techniques, as well as having each other's families accept this sudden addition. This will probably take years, not weeks or months, to accomplish. For my family, I went from just one child to four in a relatively short amount of time, and they were not prepared or ready for this change. They now had three more children to plan for birthdays, holidays and family gatherings.

You would think, the more the merrier, especially when children are involved, but this was a battle I had to fight for the first few years. My daughter had been the only baby and was easily spoiled by my family. They had a hard time accepting three more children, especially not being by blood relation. You would think these little children would all be welcomed with open arms, but that is just not how all family dynamics are. Again, everybody needs time to adjust and bond. It also takes time for extended families to know or realize that this new family unit is a long-term or permanent situation. People seem to have a hard time investing their hearts, energy and finances into something that may be temporary or short-lived. Unlike children who are born into the family, if the couple does break up, then everyone is in jeopardy of losing these relationships just as quickly as they began.

After a couple of years together and not allowing my family to treat any of our children any differently, they were finally loved as part of the family. It is important to remember that, as a step-parent, you never completely take the place of their birth parent, regardless if the other parent is involved or not. I was just blessed to be another maternal support in these children's lives. The same goes for my husband as he became another father figure to my daughter, and they developed that bond as well. Along with the many blessings of building our families together, there were several years of hard times as well. Some things I handled pretty well and others that I could have done much better.

One of the most difficult challenges when blending a family with children is the parenting and custody arrangements. As a step-parent, you get to make all the same sacrifices any other parent would, if not more, yet you do not get the same privileges or rights as the biological parent. It is very important to know this and be okay with it. There are court hearings and parenting times scheduled that you will probably not have the final say in, if any at all. And, even though you may be raising the children more days in your home, the court might not even let you into the hearings. Basically, as the spouse and step-parent, your role is really to be a loving support system for your new family. You will have very little control of anything outside of your home. Many times, I would be in the background expressing what I thought should or shouldn't happen when my husband was on the phone discussing things with his ex. This does not help the situation in any way. Even though you will have many valid concerns and opinions of your own, the battle really belongs to your spouse when it comes to their children. Besides, for me, I had my own custody arrangements to take care of.

I know, in defense, whatever outcomes happen will affect you. The arrangements your spouse and their ex-spouse make will impact your emotions, schedule and finances. Deciding to be part of a blended family is not for the faint of heart or those who feel they need to be in control at all times, which I struggle with both. This does not mean that you cannot express your concerns or opinions, but it should be primarily discussed privately with your spouse. It is important to discuss what you want and hope for, but realize that you may not get exactly what you want, and neither will your spouse.

There are a lot of negotiations and compromises that are made throughout the years of raising step-children. One side does not usually get everything they want, so you must be flexible. Most importantly, pray and pray some more for the outcome to be what is truly best for the children in each situation. These times are very hard for children whose parents are divorced, and their little worlds have been turned upside down. They go from having one home with both of their parents to bouncing between multiple homes and additional parents if they remarry. The foundation of their security has shifted, and now they are in the crossfires of custody battles and shared parenting time. And with the court system now having the final say as to the fate of their future if the parents don't come to an agreement on their own. Unfortunately, many parents even start using their own children as pawns to retaliate against their exes. But this is the most important time for you to show as much love and stability as you can while building a new foundation amidst the chaos.

Now, to those who have not been through a divorce where children are involved or have not been remarried, you probably think, why not just stay married or wait until your children are grown before separating? But we can even turn to the Bible to see the significant role that adoptive or step-parents play in the life of a child. For example, Moses was placed in a basket and sent down the river by his mother to protect him from Pharaoh. A lovely woman found him and raised him as her own, and God used him to lead the Israelites out of slavery in Egypt. Jesus was not even conceived by a man, so He was raised by His mother's husband, Joseph. He took care of Him as his son, and Jesus became the Messiah of the whole world. Now, God has adopted us as His own children, and we have become heirs to all of His promises and blessings through Jesus Christ. When we take part in raising any children, whether from our own lineage or from another's, we make an impact in that child's life for years to come. It is up to us whether we will choose to have a positive or negative effect on their life. As I stated in a previous chapter, I had a stepmother who seemed to love me at first and then despised me and still does to this day. It was horrible to live through that rejection, and it tormented me for years. But I hope that it influenced me to be the best stepmom I could be to my own stepchildren.

I have so many amazing memories as a blended family when our children were younger, despite all the challenges. We took them camping and on bike rides throughout the city. We made a tradition of going to Great Wolf Lodge for Christmas several years in a row, which they now do with their own children. We also had a family vacation home where we spent the summers swimming and enjoying the sand dunes. The most important influence that I am grateful to have was the years I took the children to church and introduced them to God. I would not have been blessed with these precious moments had I not made a commitment to be one family, all blended together. And now my daughter has siblings that she still considers her brother and sisters to this day.

Life Lessons

- Today, nearly half of all marriages end in divorce, even within the church.
- Most adults who have divorced eventually remarry, and many of them have children from previous marriages.
- Nowadays, blended families or adopted children are

just as commonplace, if not more, than traditional families who have both parents living in one household.

- God loves all of His children and cares very much for each of them, so let's equally care for each one, whether birthed or adopted as our own.

Prayer: *Lord, we thank You for the blessing of children and ask for Your strength and wisdom to care for them as You have cared for us as Your very own. Amen.*

Declaration: *God knew me before He formed me in the womb and chose me before I was born (Jeremiah 1:5).*

CHAPTER 7

FORGIVE & FORGET

"Love covers all sins" (Proverbs 10:12, NKJV).

When I was around twenty-six years old, I decided to quit my full-time job to take care of our four young children. They were having a hard time in daycare, and my heart's desire was to have more time to raise them. It was important to me to bond with them, guide them and teach them whatever I could as a mother while I still had the chance. This decision was not previously discussed with my husband, but I had reached my breaking point and needed to come home. I now realize that making that tremendous leap of faith was not only good for our family, but it was also the start of my own healing journey. In those days, I lived very much in the world and in my own flesh, but God showed up again. This time, He came as my restorer, redeemer and healer. He wanted to start putting back together everything in me that had been broken. My healing journey took many, many years, but this was when it started.

For an entire year, He started revealing to me that the first step towards my recovery and peace was my willingness to forgive all of those who had hurt me in my life. I realize that some traumas are so deep or still too fresh that forgiveness seems impossible or even unwarranted. I understand how it seems much easier to stay in the bitterness and resentment that we hold onto as a form of protection from further heartbreak, but there is so much more freedom available when we choose to forgive. I will share with you what God revealed to me about what forgiveness actually means, why we must do it in order to heal, how to implement it in our lives and the blessings that come from our obedience in doing so.

At this time in my life, I was still filled with so much anger and hatred towards the many people who had betrayed and hurt me in my past. I remember most of my time driving, I would be listening to heavy metal music on full blast on the radio while speeding down the road. It was one of the ways I knew how to release all the pent-up anger and frustrations I had inside of me. I wasn't really on speaking terms with my dad, my stepmom still despised me, plus I had all the pressures of work, raising children and focusing on my marriage. I had been smoking marijuana and cigarettes every day for the past several years just to maintain some sort of peace within. I was definitely living in victim mentality mode, which I felt I had every right to do. I had my own pity party daily, where I was always the guest of honor. The thing I hadn't realized was that we miss the abundant life God wants us to have when we choose to hang onto all those resentments associated with the wrongs done to us. There is a price for choosing to live in the pain of our past, and it's called bondage. The only problem is that we are the captives, not our enemies.

Well, one day, as I was cleaning the house while my husband was at work and the children were at school, Joyce Meyer came on the television. It was the first time in my life that I heard her preaching, and she happened to be teaching about forgiveness. The first thing I had to learn was what forgiveness was and what it wasn't. Forgiveness is simply the decision we make in our hearts and minds to no longer hold resentment towards the person or persons who have offended or hurt us. And when you release that offense, amazingly, the most important person you actually set free is yourself. Forgiveness does not mean that you have to let that person continue hurting you or even be in your life if it is toxic or abusive. You can still acknowledge the pain as you heal, but you are merely choosing to no longer harbor the resentment associated with that offense or the offender.

You may ask, why should I let the guilty go unpunished as if they did nothing wrong? So, let us examine why. As simply as I can put it, God has forgiven us even though we are guilty as well. Through the most selfless act in history, Jesus died an excruciating death upon a cross so that we would be found blameless in the eyes of God. We are now justified as though we have never sinned. Jesus bore all of our sins as His own so that we would have no penalty for them. Basically, our Creator died to save His own creation. Who would do that but a most loving and merciful God? With just one word, He could have chosen to destroy us just as quickly as He created us, but instead, He chose to redeem us through forgiveness. So, even though God owes us nothing, He gave His very own Son.

Can you imagine being willing to die for someone who hated or cursed you? Yet, in Romans 5:8, Paul tells us that while we were still sinners, Christ died for us. He did not wait until we apologized and asked for forgiveness. Otherwise, His plan would still not be fulfilled if it were dependent on us. The same goes for us forgiving others. We cannot wait until they apologize or maybe feel remorse for what they have done because many never will. Also, Jesus tells us that unless we forgive those who offend us, our Father in heaven will not forgive us. I believe since God made the ultimate sacrifice to extend His forgiveness to us, He feels very strongly that we should do the same.

Once I learned what forgiveness was and why it is so significant, now I had to learn how to apply this to my own life. Again, this whole process took me a year and continues to this day. And since forgiveness sounds simpler than it really is, I decided to start with the easiest offenses first. This category of people may have included past coworkers, acquaintances, a customer who had been rude or maybe the guy who cut me off in traffic. These were the people that I didn't have much of a relationship with, knew very well or possibly would never see again. There was not a lot of dependence on these relationships or history with them, but I still remembered what they had done or said to offend me and held a grudge. As easily as I was offended or irritated back then, that initial list probably had quite a few people on it to work through.

I was able to get through forgiving these people for seemingly petty offenses pretty quickly, realizing that they, being human like me, probably didn't even know they had upset me. Once I got through that list of offenses, it was time to go a little deeper into the wounds that caused more severe pain or turmoil in my life. This was not as easy, so I had to work through one person at a time. Again, the easiest ones first, until I felt I had truly forgiven each one of them in my heart.

I started with family members who had protected my dad or his wife instead of protecting me. I forgave my mom for not being as nurturing as I had needed growing up. I forgave my ex-husband for his abusive treatment towards me. I just kept working through each one until I got near the end of the list, to the few who had caused me the most amount of pain. It was getting easier as I had some practice on forgiving now, and I was able to forgive my dad, realizing that he, too, was raised in a dysfunctional family and had his own past wounds. I finally found forgiveness for my stepmom, but the process did not happen overnight. I had to repeatedly say I forgive you every day in my heart and mind until I could feel the wounds heal. But as I kept repeating this process every day, it got easier and easier. It was like giving up any addiction in which every day that you move further away from holding onto the offense, the less of a grip it has on you.

Sometimes, the hardest person to forgive is yourself. In the last public interview with Johnny Cash, he was asked if he had any regrets. He said that he used to but he forgave himself because when he realized that God forgave him, he figured he better do it too. I have had so many regrets that I would dwell on them so much, which kept me stuck in my past. Especially how I should have, could have or would have done so many things differently. Eventually, you have to let that go, too. For one, the reality is that what's done is done, and you cannot go back to change any of it. Bethenny Frankel said that one of the greatest pieces of advice she received from Ellen DeGeneres is that you will keep repeating the same mistakes until you actually learn the lesson. It is true, and I have made some of the same mistakes over and over again, hoping that each time, I would get it right. But if not, I will receive God's forgiveness and grace so that I can continue moving forward.

Now, I did not call a single person regarding any of these offenses and tell them that I forgave them. They would have probably hung up on me or could have just as well told me of the many things I did to them. This was just me making a choice to move forward with my life and stop looking back at all the painful things I felt were done wrong to me. We will never get very far down the road if we are constantly looking in the rearview mirror. I was so happy with the peace and freedom I was feeling from going through this healing process, and I was becoming more and more content in my everyday life. Now, I did not expect God to add any supernatural miracles to this process, but He did. This was one of those moments when you know that God and only God could have done that.

Shortly after going through this healing journey, doors of opportunities started opening up, relationships started mending and reconciliations were taking place. Sometimes, it was me who initiated contact, or someone reached out to me. But the most surprising thing that happened was when we received an unexpected phone call from my step-mom. She suddenly wanted to have a relationship with us and our children. I had not contacted her, nor would I have dared. This was when I knew God had been at work behind the scenes and was preparing my heart and even those who I was privately forgiving. In Matthew 6:4, God reminds us that when we do good in secret, He will reward us openly for all to see. This was one of those times.

Of course, forgiveness is not a one-and-done process. I had just released all the anger and resentment that had been built up over many years, but we will always have new opportunities to forgive because people will still be imperfect for the rest of our lives. Sometimes, you will find that you have to forgive the same people on several occasions, especially the ones you are in the closest relationship with. There will always be another person who cuts you off in traffic or doesn't hold the door open for you when going into the grocery store. And, many times, we will be the person who needs to be forgiven because we make mistakes too.

Lastly, some of us need to forgive God, and that is okay. He is big enough to handle the fact that we feel He has let us down in some way. Sometimes, it is hard for us to understand how a loving and powerful God could allow all the hurts and pains we endure in this world. I wish I had the answer to that, but I do know that He never intended for us to live this way. His Word is full of promises and hope that He does have a good plan for us, even though it doesn't always make sense or is easy to understand. As we grow in our relationship with Jesus Christ, we will find that He is with us, He is for us, and He can comfort us in the midst of our pain.

Life Lessons

- God sent His only Son to die for our sins so that we may be forgiven, so He rightfully commands us to forgive people for the things that have been done to us.

- Forgiveness is not based on a feeling, but it is a decision. Yet feelings of peace and joy will eventually follow.

- To forgive does not mean to excuse or allow offenses or abuse to continue or not to seek justice for criminal acts. Or reconciliation if doing so causes you or others to be put in danger. God forgives us but does not enable or condone bad behavior.

- The only way to heal and be set free from bitterness and resentment is to forgive those who have hurt you. Otherwise, the offenses you hold will only continue to hurt you.

- We, ourselves, will always need forgiveness from others and from God, so we must be willing to forgive as well. The Bible says that those who have been forgiven much love much, so choose love.

Prayer: *Lord, thank You for the forgiveness and mercy that we do not deserve, and help us to extend that same grace and mercy to others. Amen.*

Declaration: *I am kind and compassionate, forgiving others as God through Christ forgave me (Ephesians 4:32).*

CHAPTER 8

LET GO & LET GOD

"For He cares for you" (1 Peter 5:7, NKJV).

Some people think that hanging on proves how strong you are, and others may think that strength is found in letting go. I believe that in everyone's journey, there are times to hang on and times to let go, and strength comes with both. The Bible says in Ecclesiastes 3 that there is a time for every activity under the heavens. This seems to also be true in knowing when to fight and when to surrender. Now, I am not saying surrender to the enemy, but in all things, trust and allow God to be in control of all the areas that you are trying to control yourself. Alanon is one support group that helps codependent people like me learn how to let go. They teach people that letting go does not mean that you stop caring but, instead, you stop enabling, taking responsibility or suffering the consequences of another person's actions or behaviors. So, instead of trying to fix those around you, you can now start working on yourself.

Letting go may be one of the hardest things to do in life. Especially since it typically consists of the painful act of releasing someone or the outcome of something that you care deeply about, even though you really want to hold on to them or make things happen according to your desires. This is true when it comes to our past and future, our hopes and dreams, our goals and plans, our failures and weaknesses and, certainly, the people we love and have relationships with. I have found that there are very few things in this life that we have control over, and even in those few things, we probably don't have as much control as we think we do. Now, I am saying that we should not live without intentionality and just throw all caution to the wind; I found the danger in that. However, as a very driven and goal-oriented person with many years of experience, I have found that God is truly the only One in control.

Let me give you some examples. It may be a relationship that you once held dear that has now changed over time due to various life circumstances. It could be something you worked really hard to get but is no longer serving a purpose in your life. Or, the simple fact that you cannot stop time and seasons change, kids grow up, loved ones pass away and every day we are getting a little older. And the list of reasons why we have to let go of certain people or things goes on and on, from relationships being abusive or toxic to people moving away or starting new adventures.

Life is constantly changing, and the sooner we realize and accept that, the sooner we can stop fighting it and allow life to flow as it is meant to be. As I mentioned in the previous chapter, we had four children, and I loved them all equally. God had put a desire in my heart that allowed me to care for my husband's children as if they were my own from the very beginning. And because of this deep love for them, one of the hardest times in my life was when we had to let go of our oldest daughter. I don't think life can fully prepare you for the journey of raising teenagers (which I feel sorry for my own parents) or the art of letting them go. I don't doubt that if you can survive these years, you can survive anything. Well, for ten years, we had four teenagers at the same time. The oldest was really the starting point of when we had to learn where to draw the battle lines and that they would be renegotiated many times along the way.

We probably were considered strict or overprotective parents. My husband and I were not raised with a lot of protection or supervision, so I think that put some fear in us that our children would do the same things we did if we let them out of our sight for too long. We were very structured with set bedtimes, tried to control what programs they watched on television and fought the ever-advancing technology era of cell phones and social media. Now, most attentive and caring parents would think this is good and should be a normal standard, and I agree. We definitely have to be aware of and guard our children against things we know could harm them. Unfortunately, we were pretty extreme at times and lacked the consideration of understanding our children's emotions and desires, not just their behaviors.

When you have four children, you have four very different personalities and four different ways each child internalizes situations and consequences. Two of our children desired to follow the rules and avoid getting into trouble (or they were just sneakier about it). They responded to this type of structure by being overachievers and believing that love and acceptance were based on performance. They feared disappointing us and became more self-disciplined. However, the other two were more free-spirited (like me) and responded to this kind of pressure by running further away and rebelling. Our strict rules and expectations caused them to feel trapped or unworthy because we didn't give them a safe place to share their feelings and struggles. It was more of a do as you're told, without any explanation, kind of environment.

As the girls got older, we were especially strict on the clothes they could wear, how much makeup was appropriate or who they could hang out with. If a boy called, my husband would pick up the phone and hang up without question. We were afraid of them going outside when we weren't home, going out with friends or to football games or having cell phones for fear something would corrupt them. What happens when you limit a child to grow or trust them with making some of their own decisions? They only want to rebel more. This caused many heated arguments within our home. The other problem we faced was that their other parents were not nearly as protective as we were and much more lenient. This resulted in our approach being more ineffective since we were considered the strict and unfair parents.

When our oldest daughter turned fifteen, she decided she would rather live with her biological mother. We were very concerned because she would not have the discipline we felt she would need to achieve the things we hoped for her. And our standards for our children weren't really much more than making sure they graduated high school without getting pregnant. But at some point, her tenacious spirit was more than we could handle, and we decided to let her go. It was very hard, but we still tried to maintain as much control as possible from a distance. Her mother promised she would make her go to school every day and keep her grades up, which she had already been struggling with. At first, everything seemed to be going okay, and they were keeping up their end of the bargain.

After a short time, we found out that she was missing

school often, her grades were failing and she was doing a lot of things we believed were unacceptable for a child her age. Our worst fears were realized, and the more we fought to get her back, the less she would even talk to us. Eventually, we found out that she was living with her boyfriend's family and no longer staying with her mother. She was sixteen, and we were running out of legal options to bring her home. My husband tried going through the court system, but there was not much they could enforce at her age. We did learn that we could take her home, although, not sure if we could make her stay. She agreed to let us take her to dinner one night, and after we ate, we pulled off into a parking lot near where she was staying and told her we were taking her home. She then whipped open the sliding door of our minivan and took off running. We met back up with her at her boyfriend's house, but by this point, we realized we had exhausted all of our efforts. It was just time to let her go; there was nothing more we could do.

We still had three children to tend to at home and had to keep things as calm as possible for them. I had been strong in my faith for a few years by this point and believed that as much as we loved her, God loved her even more, so we could trust that He would protect her. It took quite some time for all of us to heal from this and get back to some normalcy. I learned that for my own sanity, I had to stop fighting the inevitable, and my faith grew stronger, realizing that God was in control, not me. There was a lot of hurt, anger and mistrust for each of us, but eventually, the door opened little by little for her to pursue a relationship with us again. Over the next few years, all our children grew up and moved out, and we had survived the child-rearing years. And one did graduate while being pregnant; what can you do? But let me tell you from the other side, those years went really fast. They are all doing very well and started their own families, and we now have many precious grandchildren. No amount of worry or sleepless nights will change the course of life, but prayer is the one thing we can truly go to. This may have been one of the first times I had to really lean on trusting God in my life, but it definitely would not be the last.

Life Lessons

- Some of our biggest battles can only be fought on our knees.
- Trusting God, regardless of the outcome, is our truest way to grow in faith.
- The Bible assures us that God is able to do more than we could ever ask or imagine and that He will work all things out for the good of those who love Him.
- Remember, as much as you care about someone or something, God cares even more.

- God is the only One truly in control, no matter how much we try to beg, plead or manipulate any situation.

Prayer: *Lord, give us the serenity to accept the things we cannot change, the courage to change the things we can and the wisdom to know the difference. Amen.*

Declaration: *I trust in the Lord with all of my heart and lean not on my own understanding (Proverbs 3:5).*

CHAPTER 9

GET A BACKBONE

"Perfect love casts out fear" (1 John 4:18, NKJV).

Because of the abuse and mistreatment in my past, I have easily allowed people to control and influence me. I did not stand up for myself often, and if I did, it was not in a healthy manner. I usually reacted out of pure emotions: crying, being defensive or screaming out of anger, to name a few. I was very passive-aggressive and definitely let my feelings have full reign. I was also sensitive and easily hurt, so my triggers were many. I needed people to be my source of approval and validation, which gave them the power to make my moods go up or down. I was always so worried that I would upset somebody, disappoint them or cause them to no longer like me because rejection was devastating to me.

I carried so much guilt and condemnation that it seemed like no matter how perfect I tried to be, I was always letting somebody down, especially God. I could not quite live up to the demands and expectations I put on myself or allowed others to put on me. I seemed to always come up short, and that type of disappointment would often leave me feeling hopeless and discouraged. And I was mentally and physically drained from constantly trying to keep up with everyone's expectations of me and what I thought would make them happy.

The problem with trying so hard to please everyone around you is that, along the way, you eventually lose yourself. I could not understand what the Bible meant in Romans 8:1 (NIV) that there is now no condemnation for those who are in Christ Jesus or Matthew 11:28 (NIV) when Jesus said come to Me, all you who are weary and burdened, and I will give you rest. How could I not feel condemned or find that kind of peace to enter into such a rest? I had to take care of everyone, even if that meant neglecting myself. In fact, that would just pile on more guilt from being selfish if I took the time to take care of my own needs before anyone else's.

This was even more true when it came to men. I fell into the peer pressures of sex as a teenager and let men treat me any way they wanted because I desperately needed their approval and attention. This pattern remained throughout both of my marriages and well into my forties. In fact, I had told my counselor at one point that all of my abusers loved me because this is what I truly believed. She paused for a moment and silently looked at the floor before looking back at me and stating that I had years of work ahead of me. Boy, was she right! This is all I knew of love. It was not until my late twenties that I really started digging into my worth according to what my Heavenly Father thought of me. This would be the start of another twenty-plus years of healing and understanding to even comprehend.

So, going back to twenty years old, I had packed up my apartment for the last time and finally left my abusive husband. I had potentially found a new man, one who might really love me. He had been betrayed in his marriage, so it only made sense to heal our wounds together. I was young and so infatuated that I could not see that I was really just trading in one dysfunctional relationship for another without considering the need for my own time to heal. My new boyfriend worked hard, was responsible and very clean, so this surely felt like a step up. To put it frankly, it's kind of like trading in your old car for a new shiny one. However, you never know what issues it has until after you actually purchase it and take it home.

I remember that for the first year of my new relationship, I would flinch whenever he raised his arms to hug me, even though he had never hit me. It was an auto-response triggered by the abuse of my previous relationship, which psychologists would probably refer to as complex post-traumatic stress disorder (C-PTSD). But even though he did not cause me physical harm, there was something

I learned very quickly from the beginning. He had a very strong, authoritative demeanor and tone and made it very clear that if he did not get his way, he would get angry. Of course, as a people pleaser, I did not want him to be upset, especially with me. So, as long as I pleased him and did what he wanted, we would get along just fine. Over time, I managed to get very skilled at reading facial expressions and body language. People would only have to give me a look or stance that they were upset or offended, and I would make sure not to ever do that again. I became a puppet on a string but with many different masters, and my second husband became the primary one.

From early on in our relationship, I felt something was wrong but didn't know what it was. I was so blinded with love and adoration for him, and since he regularly reminded me of all the things wrong with me, I figured it was me. But one of the clues that made me think that maybe there was more to the issue than me just being sensitive or emotional was that I was a pretty bubbly and fun person most of the time while I was at work, laughing and joking with my coworkers all day, but I would feel this sense of dread going home. Even my demeanor would completely change to a timid and downcast attitude.

This may be a huge clue for you if you are in a similar situation. And I am not talking about the occasional bad day being overwhelmed thinking about your responsibilities at home but an actual fear or anxiousness knowing that you are going back into a distressing situation. You can ask yourself some of the following questions as well. Are you excited or happy to go home, or do you dread walking through the door? Do you feel fear, anxiety or depression thinking about being near your partner on a regular basis? If so, this could be a sign that you are in a toxic or abusive relationship. Some people may wonder, how can you not know that you are in an abusive relationship? Well, I was in this marriage for sixteen years and didn't realize the extent of what I was dealing with for fifteen of them.

Verbal and emotional abuse can be a lot more insidious and difficult to detect than physical abuse, whereas physical abuse leaves visible marks and bruises that leave a trace of evidence. And even with physical abuse, victims who stay do not fully understand what is going on, and so they justify the behavior, even as it escalates. The thing about abuse is that the relationship is not always bad or seemingly harmful. In fact, in the beginning, it can be one of the most loving and fulfilling relationships you ever had. Habitual abusers are known to use a technique called love bombing, where they appear to be everything you ever wanted with their charm and promises of a wonderful future together.

Unfortunately, unbeknownst to their victim, all this flattery is just a form of manipulation to earn their trust and gain power and control in the relationship. Then, while they have them in this state of ecstasy, their true colors start to show, leaving their victim in a state of confusion and panic. As they grasp to reclaim the wonderful person they fell for, they do not realize this person never truly existed. Later in this chapter, I will share with you the many behaviors and techniques that abusive people use to gain power and control in the relationship.

Now, regarding my second marriage, I did not need much love bombing because I was instantly head over heels at basically hello, so he didn't have to use much charm. I was just completely naïve about what was considered healthy or unhealthy behaviors in a relationship because I never knew what healthy boundaries were. But we had a lot of blessings and fun times over the course of our marriage. He wasn't always mean or critical, just often enough to keep me on my toes and tear down my self-esteem. This makes abuse quite confusing because you don't know what is real and what isn't. He showed me love and affection, but I always felt that I had to earn it to keep it.

I thought for years that if I showed him how much I loved him, eventually, he would truly love me back. I hoped that the more I gave, the more his heart would change.

But it ended up being the more I gave, the more he took. The relationship was always lacking in equality, as I had to fight for my rights and voice over the years. Looking back, the times we had the best seasons in our marriage were when I was the one giving and serving without expecting anything in return. I would dote over him and do all that I could to make him feel valued, only to be devalued in the process. Whenever I would pull back my efforts after being hurt or exhausted from being the only one giving all the time, he still never reciprocated.

Being a Christian woman in my faith and taught how the Bible says we are to submit and obey our husbands, I did just that. And he absolutely loved me when I did, so it made sense that I hoped this would also win him over to God someday. Instead, he continued being harsh, demanding and critical of our children and me most of the time. Every time we tried to reach his standards, it seemed like he would just move the bar on us. We never felt good enough, no matter how hard we tried. I could only cook the kinds of foods he liked, and even then, my meals were often criticized. I tried to keep up with his sexual needs, only to be called a prude when I wasn't in the mood. When I did give in, sometimes I would cry during sex because I felt no emotional bond, so I just felt used and empty inside. The relationship was very detrimental to my emotional and mental health and further confirmed my belief that love had to be earned through our works. I had always viewed God the same way, so I would beat myself up for any of my failures and shortcomings.

I did not have a safe place to speak up or share my feelings, and not just because I would sometimes get an angry response, but often, no response at all. When I usually would cry out for resolution or real intimacy in our relationship, all I would get was his back turned against me, and he would walk away. One of the reasons it took me so long to figure out how neglectful and damaging the relationship was was that he never hit me physically, only with words, and never called me names. But he would tell me all the time that I was sensitive and overdramatic and that all of his hurtful criticisms were just jokes. And I didn't find them funny because I have no sense of humor, even though he was the only one laughing. And because I knew I had issues, I believed that it was me, so I took all the blame upon myself, just as I always had since childhood.

When I worked full-time, he would remind me that I was inadequate because I could not keep up with all of the household chores, cooking or his sexual needs. If I was a stay-at-home mom to tend more to the house, kids and his needs, then I was insufficient for not working. This caused so much of my anxiety and depression to escalate over the years, more than I had already struggled with due to my own deficiencies. I feared being at work while the kids were home with him, even for an hour, because I wanted to be home to care for them. In fact, I mainly stayed in the relationship for the last ten years to protect my step-children because there was no way I could leave them to fend for themselves, and I didn't want him to crush their spirits without me being around to try to rebuild them.

Halfway through our marriage, I finally began sticking up for myself. I started reading books to help in every area of my life, including setting appropriate boundaries, changing my thoughts and knowing my worth, to name a few. At first, this only made my husband more upset because he started losing control over me, but once he saw that I was no longer backing down, he started backing off. The thing with people who have a bully mentality is that they only have as much power as you allow them until you call their bluff. I finally gained more freedom and power to express myself, but we never got to a place where there was genuine love and equality. I had finally accepted that my husband was not capable of loving our children and me the way a father and husband should. This was when I found myself mourning the relationship that I had hoped and prayed for from the beginning, which continued for the last three years of our marriage.

After fifteen years together, most of our children were grown and had moved out. We only had my daughter left at home, and it was her senior year of high school. One of my aunts handed me a book called *The Verbally Abusive Relationship* by Patricia Evans. The first time I tried reading it, it hit me so hard and brought me back to all the earlier years when our children were younger and I didn't know enough to protect them better. I couldn't face the truth, so I set it down. Six months later, I finally had the courage to read it.

This time, I couldn't put it down, and I finally got the answers that I had long waited for. However, it wasn't what I wanted or expected to hear, but it was the cold, hard truth. I had been verbally abused all of these years. To say that I had been abused by my husband and refer to him as abusive seemed so harsh to me. He had shown me love as best as he knew how, so I always had compassion for him. But I could not deny the fact that he had used almost every technique in the book to control and manipulate me during our entire relationship. He would often lie, criticize, deny, blame shift, project, judge and use guilt trips to get whatever he wanted. He was the type of person who was very insensitive to the feelings of others yet very sensitive in regard to his own feelings.

There were many times I felt like I was going crazy because the things I was told were true were actually untrue, or what was untrue was really true. This form of abuse is called gaslighting. This type of psychological warfare is where a person trying to control another person attempts to cause self-doubt and confusion, leaving their victim to question their own judgment. They will use any weapon they have to gain and keep power and control so that they can satisfy their own needs and agenda, regardless of how it hurts others. They do not take responsibility for their actions or sincerely apologize for their hurtful behaviors. Typically, the only time they appear to apologize or show remorse is when they need to keep you in their vicious cycle so that you don't leave them. This is just another form of manipulation because they do not have any intention to actually change their abusive behaviors.

When it comes to habitual abusers, the only ones that truly matter to them are themselves. Their main objective is to advance their own agenda, and they do not see the world like most people who strive for fairness and equality. Very few abusive people change because most will not acknowledge that they have a problem because their self-esteem is too low to accept that they even have an issue. And the few that do admit to their abuse will not get the help they need or willing to put in the work needed to change. Unfortunately, the majority of abusers will just continue to victimize anyone and everyone in their path. So, if you or someone you know is in this situation, please seek professional and experienced abuse counseling to help consider your best and safest options available.

I knew I wanted to be free from this toxic and abusive relationship, but I still wasn't strong enough to have the courage to say it aloud. I was afraid of so many things, like confronting him, hurting the children, disappointing God or the stigma of another divorce. These fears led me to do the worst thing I could have imagined, and I prayed for what I thought was the easiest way out, that he would just die. It wasn't long after that when my husband started complaining of chest pains, and we assumed it was just indigestion; that was until he collapsed in the driveway. He suffered a massive heart attack in the ambulance on the way to the hospital, and thankfully, they saved his life. But I felt so much guilt and remorse, thinking he almost died because of me. I didn't really want him dead or our children without a father; I just wanted to be free from the abuse.

I was a God-fearing, praying Christian woman, even in the times that my story did not reflect that. But I thought God would eventually change him. The only thing God changed was me. He gave me the knowledge to know the truth, the courage to stand up for myself and the strength to leave. Within one year of reading that book, trying to use the proper techniques on how to respond to his abusive behaviors and set healthier boundaries, I had finally had enough.

I am grateful that I was finally free and able to spend the next several years rebuilding my self-esteem and my relationship and understanding of God and His love for me, which I learned I never had to strive to earn or be good enough for. I now have a whole new level of confidence that I could have never achieved if I had stayed in that situation, which constantly crushed my spirit. The Bible repeatedly warns of the effects and influence of being around certain types of people. I didn't know that I had rights or that I had given them away. Now, I am able to determine where to set my boundaries and when I want to say yes or no.

It didn't happen overnight, but every day, I got a little bit stronger and more independent. It took all of my strength the first year not to run back to that which was comfortable and familiar. My family was split apart, and I had to go through the long, agonizing process of grieving and healing over that. For the first three years after I left, I still prayed for restoration and reconciliation, but he never changed. After all I had learned the following several years after my second divorce, I still continued to fall into abusive relationships, which only pushed me further into my healing journey. God is continually healing the brokenness that has allowed me to be so vulnerable to abusive and toxic relationships for most of my life, and I continue striving to become a better version of myself each and every day. We are stronger than we realize, and even though it's hard, our life is worth fighting for. When the fear of staying outweighs the fear of leaving, we find our way out. God will make a way where there seems to be no way. The following is a summary I wrote from the book by Patricia Evans on verbal abuse to help understand what abuse is.

Verbal Abuse—Any words or attitudes that disempower, disrespect or devalue another person.

Abuser—Anyone who uses words or behaviors to control or manipulate another person.

Victim—A person who has had their rights or boundaries violated, often causing them emotional or mental suffering.

Forms of Abuse—Accusing, blaming, blocking, countering, crazy-making, criticizing, denial, discounting, diverting, forgetting, gaslighting, judging, manipulating, name-calling, ordering, sarcasm disguised as jokes, threatening, trivializing, undermining, withholding.

Victim's Feelings—Anxiety, confusion, depression, disappointment, fear, frustration, guilt, hurt, hopelessness, inadequacy, rejection, sadness, shame, shock.

Basic Rights—Respect and courtesy of feelings, views and ideas; freedom from any kind of abuse; and emotional support.

Proper Responses to Verbal Abuse—Firmly say, "Stop it," or "Do not speak to me that way." Remove yourself from the situation, if necessary. Do not defend yourself, argue or debate with an abuser. Never try to justify, rationalize or take ownership of another's abusive behavior. Remember, verbal abuse is a violation, not a conflict, and should never be tolerated.

"If you experience the slightest feeling that something is wrong, it is" (Patricia Evans).

"Sticks and stones may break our bones, but words will break our hearts" (Robert Fulghum).

Life Lessons

- God created marriage to be an intimate and honorable life-long covenant between a man and a woman. He instructs the man to love his wife as himself and the wife to respect her husband. Love is respectful, and respect is an act of love.
- Proverbs tells us not to make friends with an easily angered man, not to even associate with them. And

that it is better to live in the wilderness than with a quarrelsome woman.

- More than 12 million women and men experience domestic violence each year from an intimate partner, 85 percent of them being female, and almost 50 percent of children in violent homes are also abused.
- Abusive behaviors only tend to escalate over time. Unless the abuser seeks professional help, which can take years to change, the percentage of recovery is very low.
- If you or someone you know is experiencing domestic abuse, please seek professional help. Abuse is never the fault of the victim, and the most dangerous time for a victim is when they are leaving their abusive partner.

Prayer: *Lord, let us not forget that You know first-hand the torment of abuse, as Your Son endured it greatly while here on this earth. We ask, in Your lovingkindness, to heal and restore all that has been lost and broken. Amen.*

Declaration: *God has not given me a spirit of fear but of power, love and a sound mind (2 Timothy 1:7).*

CHAPTER 10

GET RID OF EVERYTHING & GET A LIFE

"He shall cover you with His feathers"
(Psalm 91:4, NKJV).

You don't have to look very far to see how prevalent materialism has become in our society. I realize that chasing possessions and putting much emphasis on the things of this world have always played a significant role in our history. However, we now have the rapid advancement of technology, commercials and social media to make us believe that we cannot live without certain products. We went from trying to keep up with the Joneses to keeping up with the Kardashians. But do you think all that money and material possessions really make us happy? How can we expect to be completely fulfilled by obtaining more stuff when, generally, it means acquiring more debt and working more hours just to get them? Plus, whatever you buy today will just be replaced with the latest and greatest gadget in a few short months, and then that will be the next big thing to get. It is a never-ending and never-fully satisfying desire to keep chasing things and their empty promises.

There were two times in my life when I had decided to get rid of everything in order to get a real life filled with passion and purpose. They are among the most blessed times of my life, and I will never regret taking those leaps of faith. I had been working for five years at a pretty busy call center when our four children were quite young, not doing very well at daycare, and life felt too busy and out of control to find true peace and contentment. My heart's desire was to quit my job and take care of our children full-time, but our finances would not allow me to do that. In fact, my husband and I still had a mound of debt acquired during our first marriages a few years before.

I knew I was emotionally and mentally stretched to my limit and had been struggling with being manic-depressive and was prescribed pills for bipolar disorder. I felt like I could no longer fight to hold onto the materialistic things that we had attained and no longer found them to be really significant compared to being more stable as a family. And I desperately wanted to create a new life for us and my sanity. One day, while on my lunch break, I just decided I was done and was instantly filled with a peace and joy I had not felt in a very long time. I did not tell my boss or any coworkers, nor did I consult with my husband first. I was literally dancing as I passed by my boss' office to walk outside with my box of belongings that I had gathered from my desk. My husband was on his break around this time, so I went directly to his work and told him that I had quit my job. Surprisingly, he wasn't the least bit mad and just chuckled. However, I am not sure if, on the inside, he was feeling the same way, but I appreciated the support and no argument.

Now, I am not proud of or suggest to anyone to just abruptly leave their job without notice. I was still living in a place of timidity, so I did not have the courage to discuss the idea with my husband or give a two-week notice to my employer. They say it is easier to receive forgiveness than permission, so I think I just opted for that approach. I had made up my mind and went for it and felt like I couldn't even stop myself if I tried. I knew at that moment all the things that would have to change, and I was willing to give up or let go of any material things for the sake of providing my family with a healthier environment. Sometimes, you just have to follow your heart, gut or instincts, regardless of the opinions or suggestions of others. I have always marched to the beat of my own drum and thought of making a new way. It wasn't always the right one, but this time, I got lucky.

I was very proactive in making proper preparations to downsize our family of six in order to live off just my husband's income. We had to move from a large, four-bed-room farmhouse out in the country to a much smaller two-bedroom apartment in town. I knew we would have to surrender both of our cars to the bank and eventually claim bankruptcy due to the amount of debt we had been paying on, but it would have taken us so many more years to pay it all back, even with us both working full-time. We were able to pay cash for an old Crown Victoria with a pretty bad oil leak, which we named the "hooptie ride," but at least it was big enough to fit four little kids in it. We had all that we needed (each other), and I was able to raise our children from home. I even prayed that we could have the children live with us full-time, and eventually, situations changed to allow us to do that.

It was summer break, so we were able to pull all the kids out of daycare. We didn't have any extra money in our budget to splurge on cable or internet, and thankfully, cell phones were not a necessity yet. We spent a lot of our time bicycling around town, doing morning workouts with Jack LaLanne on a local television station and hanging out with friends and family. Many Saturdays, I would go to the lo-cal faith-based food pantry for assistance with some of our grocery needs. And sometimes, I would take the children to serve there to give back to the community. This new transition was a start for a very peaceful and happy time for us, just as I had hoped and prayed. It made my heart happy that I was able to be more physically and mentally available for my husband and our children at all times. This was also a time when I was able to start my own healing process and get back into my faith in God since I had more time and energy.

At the end of the summer, when the kids went back to school, I was able to get a part-time job close to home in order to help with finances and still maintain a slower-paced schedule that allowed me to be available when everyone got home in the evenings. One day, while the kids and I were on a bicycle ride, I saw a "for rent" sign out front of a single-family house only a few blocks away from our current apartment. I called the number listed as soon as we got home, and the homeowner was a sweet, elderly man who said it was still available. So we all piled into the "hooptie ride" to meet with him and see the house. The home had four bedrooms and was located on a large property within the same block where our kids went to school. It even had walking trails and a creek behind it. Now, mind you, we were a blended family with a bankruptcy and now living on one full-time income. Clearly, the odds were not really for us, but thankfully, we have a God who doesn't adhere to odds but moves in favor.

The landlord let us all freely go inside the house and

check it out. We didn't realize that while we were inside the house, he was looking inside our car. And because it was very neat and clean, he let us rent the house very affordably. He fell in love with us, especially our children, and even blessed us with new flooring in the kitchen and an attached garage built onto the back. I was so overwhelmed with all of the blessings that God had granted after taking the risk of losing a substantial amount of income and choosing to follow the desires of my heart instead of the fears brought on by materialism.

At this time, my part-time job was at a local bakery, and one day at work, while in a private conversation with God, I asked Him why He was being so good to me. Immediately, as I turned around, I saw a three-tier wedding cake that I had not previously noticed. There was a scripture written in frosting that said, "Delight yourself in the Lord, and he will give you the desires of your heart" (Psalm 37:4, ESV). At that moment, my heart was so overwhelmed with joy because I knew God had answered me.

Over the years, as the children got older, we rebuilt our credit, and I went back to full-time employment. We then decided to buy our first house, where we lived until our last child graduated high school. Fast forward a few more years to 2018, when I turned forty years old. Now, some would say this is about the age when some start having a mid-life crisis, but I believe I had a mid-life awakening. Regardless, I found myself in a similar situation that I had fifteen years prior. I was exhausted and burnt out at another stressful office job; my boyfriend of two years had broken up with me and my heart was shattered. I was trying so hard to hold on to all that was deemed normal and acceptable by society's standards. I was single, alone and had the only sole income to provide for myself, but I felt there was something more calling me again. I believed that there had to be a better way than working my life away just to make ends meet, and I was willing to do whatever it took to find it. Also, at this time, God had already given me this book to write years prior, and I strongly felt the time was now to fulfill that mission.

As a free-spirited minimalist, I knew that time and energy wasted is something we never get back, and I wanted to live a life with more meaning and purpose than the work-home, work-home routine that leaves us with little to no energy for much else. I had dreams to pursue, and I figured that if I was going to get free, there was no better time than now. Being on my own and debt-free, I really had nothing to lose yet possibly so much more to gain. Thankfully, I am able to somewhat balance between emotionalism and logic, so even though I tend to follow a lot of my feelings, I have always been very responsible in coming up with strategic action plans. I wanted to stay independent, but I was going to have to put some dependency on people and a lot on God. I saved all the money that I could before quitting my job, sold almost everything I owned except what was essential and planned on giving up my beautiful apartment near the lake to live out of a vehicle as the most cost-effective way to survive without an income.

When I decided this would be the best opportunity for me to accomplish some of my visions and dreams, I had only a few months to prepare. I planned everything out, from the dates I would quit my job and leave my apartment to how much money I would have saved. I created the budget I needed to live for a year being houseless. I had watched blogs and videos on how others were living out of their vehicles or motorhomes. And, yes, there is such a thing called the van life, and it is growing ever more popular as people are choosing to live free from the standard American dream of owning a house with a white picket fence. I also called my closest friends and family members with my plan of being houseless and asked for their support by opening their homes to me if I needed a place to sleep or hang out. My gypsy spirit was truly emerging.

I started a gym membership for only ten dollars a month, as getting healthy was one of my goals to accomplish during this time. Plus, they were open twenty-four hours with shower access in case I needed it. The only other bills I would have to pay every month were for my prepaid cell phone service and car insurance. Therefore, a budget of approximately $500 a month should be able to cover my bills and living expenses. I considered the option of getting a storage unit so that when I settled back down again, I would have all my things, but I wanted to be really free, with no strings attached to anything. And I wasn't afraid to start over again as I had done many times before. Plus, letting go of my old things would allow me to be open to new ideas and styles later.

I ended up leaving my job and apartment a month earlier than anticipated and did not have as much money as I wanted in my savings, but I knew this journey would have to be mostly based on faith, courage and a little strategy. Even if everything wouldn't go as expected, maybe it could be better. Besides, I learned to see life as an adventure, and even though the unknown can be scary, it can also be thrilling. I have realized time and time again that God does His best work when we release all of our fears, hopes and plans to trust in His perfect will. So, I didn't start out as perfectly as I had intended, but I knew my dreams were just on the other side of anything I feared, so I was ready to take that leap of faith.

The first thing I was praying for and needed to replace was my seventeen-year-old SUV with something more practical and versatile for my new lifestyle. I am an avid researcher, so I knew all of my options and the pros and cons of each one. Some people live in an RV, which I would love someday, but my budget was not feasible to get one with cash, and living in a campground all summer would cost just as much as my apartment. I considered a full-size conversion van, which can be super cool with interior running lights, a television and a back seat that turns into a bed. Although it was pretty spacious to live out of, it would not have been as fuel-efficient to drive around daily.

I needed something decent on gas, front-wheel drive for winter and stow-and-go seats for functionality in case I needed room for a bed if I did not have anywhere to stay at night, but also the option to fit my four grandkids if I took them somewhere. I need options in life. I love options. I finally found what I was looking for and got a well-maintained 2007 Dodge Grand Caravan. It had tinted windows so you could barely see in the back, automatic dual slider doors, a sunroof and a DVD player. It was perfect and even more than I could have hoped for. When the seats were up, there was so much room for storage. And when I put the seats down, I could use a portable mattress for a bed. Plus, I had plenty of room for the little bit of clothes and other belongings that I chose to keep.

Now that the details were in place, my other concern was how I was going to accomplish my goals during the short time I would have before my income ran out or the next winter would arrive. I spent time with God and asked Him how I could be efficient with my time and not get distracted. Literally, at that moment, I got a message from a friend asking me if I knew what a dream board was, and I realized that God had given me another answer. In case you do not know what a dream or vision board is, it is simply a bulletin board you create with pictures and sayings with your goals and dreams on it, and usually, hang it somewhere that you will see it regularly as a way to keep you inspired and motivated to achieve them. Well, I was going to be living out of my minivan, so I had nowhere to hang this board, but I still created one. To me, it was more of an act of faith or a way of putting my dreams down and trusting God to work these plans out. In fact, I put two scriptures on my board. The first from Jeremiah 29:11 (NIV), which I had been carrying around with me for almost twenty years, says, "'For I know the plans I have for you,' declares the Lord, 'plans to prosper you and not to harm you, plans to give you a hope and a future.'" I had decided that this was God's part, and I would leave that in His hands. Then, the other scripture was my responsibility, from Mark 9:23 (ESV), which says, "All things are possible for one who believes." I just had to believe that God was capable of fulfilling all the dreams He had put in my heart and the purpose He planned for my life.

The next thing I put on my board were pictures of all that I wanted to accomplish, which included writing this book, spending time in nature, losing weight, preaching the gospel and starting my professional organizing business. I even added my lifelong dream of swimming with dolphins, hoping God would maybe bless me with some time within the next few years. As it turned out, He did have a plan, and He was more than capable of seeing it through. I started the first week of what I call my nine-month sabbatical with one of my friends, a nutritionist whose house was built to accommodate taking in several people at a time. We cleaned up my diet, and I very quickly lost twenty-five pounds as well as quit smoking cigarettes. That felt amazing since I was a hundred pounds overweight at the beginning of this journey. Then, I was invited (for free) to ride down to Atlanta with one of my aunts, and while I was there, I went to their famous aquarium and got to touch a dolphin for the first time in my life.

I received professional training and launched my organizing business, took opportunities to help with a couple of local ministries that help urban youth stay on track for success and spent a lot of time in nature, especially with my new kayak. But my greatest accomplishment was writing this book. I had to wait seven years from the time God gave it to me to fulfill this dream. At the beginning of my sabbatical, I spent five days in a campground and wrote the first five chapters. Then, for the last several weeks of my time off, I was asked to house-sit for another aunt while she and her husband went on vacation. It was a beautiful house overlooking a large, secluded lake, two and a half miles down a dirt road and thirty minutes from the nearest town. The only life around me was the kitties I was taking care of, the birds, chipmunks, occasional deer, and possible bears in the woods.

Although it was beautiful, it was one of the scariest times for me. I was alone in the middle of nowhere for three weeks. As soon as it started getting dark, I would grab the cats and hide under the blankets until the sun came up. But I did get the other fourteen chapters done. I finished the book the day before they got home, and I can still remember the feeling of finally having it accomplished. The excitement, the happy dance with one of the cats in the kitchen and then sheer panic, realizing that everyone would now know all about me. But God did it! He fulfilled His promise, a long-awaited dream, plus a few bonuses along the way. I even got to go on another trip, all expenses paid, to Florida and actually swam with the dolphins. I don't think we can ever quite comprehend how good God is and how much He loves us, but He never stops doing it.

I felt so blessed to have the few things that I kept, the opportunities that I was able to take and the accomplishments that I made. Sometimes, less is more. Actually, Jesus tells His disciples in Matthew 8:20 (NIV) that "foxes have dens and birds have nests, but the Son of Man has no place to lay his head." Christ was homeless; He was on a mission, and He had a purpose to fulfill. Of course, we do not have to be homeless to follow Jesus, but it is a humbling reality when we think about it. My mission at that time was to live life without bounds, focus on my relationship with God and fulfill the purposes that I believed He had ordained.

Life Lessons

- There will always be risks in order to receive a reward, but there is never a reward without taking some risks.
- Life is short, and you cannot take all the things you've acquired with you when it's over, so choose to make more memories rather than just more money.
- Abraham Lincoln said, "In the end, it's not the years in your life that count. It's the life in your years." And Franklin Roosevelt stated, "The only thing we

have to fear is fear itself."

- Life is an adventure; live it and learn from it, but don't fear it. The only way to accomplish your dreams is to tenaciously pursue them.

Prayer: *Lord, help us not to hold so tightly to the things of this world but rather cling to You as You fulfill the desires and purpose You placed in our hearts and lives. Amen.*

Declaration: *God is my refuge and my fortress, in whom I trust (Psalm 91:2).*

CHAPTER 11

PERFECT SIMPLICITY

"For this is the love of God" (1 John 5:3, NKJV).

I was born a perfectionist. My grandma would tell stories about how I would align everybody's shoes in the entryway just perfectly, pair by pair, at only two years old. So, you could say that my perfectionism runs deep. This is one area of my life that has always been challenging to find a healthy balance. My brain interprets things in such a way that my eyes catch every detail and automatically wants to fix any imperfection, and this is true when it comes to things and people. I am the type of person who will notice almost instantly if something is out of place, such as a picture that is just slightly crooked on the wall, the drapes aren't hanging evenly or a cupboard door is open a little bit. In fact, people have been known to move or turn things to face the opposite direction on purpose to see how quickly I would notice and then fix it.

In my home, there is a place for everything, and everything is in its place. Every piece of décor or furniture is precisely chosen to match and complement each room, including the air freshener and bottle of soap. Shopping can be difficult because I am not only limited by the color selection but finding a scent I actually like as well. Once I find the acceptable color and scent, I have to make sure that the spray nozzle or any containers are set perfectly in place and pointing in a specific direction. I am also one of those who firmly believe that there is a correct way to put the toilet paper roll on the spindle, and I will fix it if it is wrong. I am not trying to be a control freak, but I tend to think that my way is the better way because I have put a lot of thought into every intricate detail.

However, I do love that I have a knack for turning any house into a home, or as some may feel when they visit, a museum where they can't touch anything. But I have used this gift (or curse) to help many other people simplify, organize and decorate their homes since I was very young. It only made sense to try and make a career out of it, and eventually, I became a professional organizer. People love coming to my house, and they tell me of the peace and calmness it makes them feel. And many people pay professionals to make their homes and lives feel this way. I love teaching people how to create a nice, simple flow throughout their homes. I believe that our world and schedules can be so hectic and full of chaos that our homes should be the one place where we can find peace and serenity. It should be a safe place where you and your family can relax at the end of a busy day and just rejuvenate and spend time together. Now, I am not saying to go to the extent of my perfectionism because that extreme can cause stress, not alleviate it, especially when living with other family members. But I can promise that your life and home will be much more carefree when you have it organized and not cluttered with excess things.

One problem I find all too common in many people's homes is that they have much more than they actually need and hardly use most of it. Why do we feel that we need to have so much stuff? And as a woman whose mind already races at a hundred miles per hour with several different thoughts at one time, I find that having my home simple and organized gives me one less area to fret about. Less stuff, less debt, less obligations means less chaos we have. Again, less is truly more: more time, more money and more freedom. Simplifying your life in every area possible allows you to create more space in your schedule, mind and life. The more clutter we have, the more there is to consume our minds.

There is so much value in learning to let go of what is unnecessary so that you're not wasting your time chasing the things that are no longer worth your time. Once you realize what is important to you, you can start letting go of all the things that are not. Just because something served a purpose in the past doesn't mean that it continues to serve a purpose now or will in the future. People change, situations change and life changes, so it is vital to accept and allow change to flow freely as the seasons change.

Looking back, I can see how much time, energy and money I wasted trying to accumulate the things that I thought made me feel important, respectable or valuable. Sometimes, we put so much value on what we look like and want others to think of us that it just becomes too high of a price to pay. I had to get real with myself and ask why I had worked so hard to obtain many of these things that I didn't even have anymore. Were actually all the things I hung onto because they were benefitting me and my current lifestyle, or was it just out of fear or pride to not let them go? These are now some of the same questions I ask my clients because we need to continually assess what is necessary at this time in our lives. Right now, you can probably think of something that you are holding onto just in case you might need it someday, even though you may not have used it in years or maybe ever.

As a minimalist, it is so freeing to have only the things I absolutely love or need in my life. And I can tell you from my own journey and experience that I found out that we do not need very much to survive or be happy. In fact, I used to think that more stuff would make me happy, but the more I let go and got rid of, the happier and more peaceful I actually became. I see this same thing while working with others who have gone through or are going through simplifying their lives. There is such a freedom when the things of this world are no longer holding you down or claiming your time that could be spent on more meaningful desires. I have been able to apply this way of thinking to most areas of my life, and like everybody else, some areas I am still working on. Sometimes, I even struggle with letting certain things go and have to ask myself, why am I keeping this? How is it benefitting me? And do I absolutely love and need it?

I also want to assure you that this is not a poor mentality mindset, either. When you actually get rid of all the things that you no longer want or use, you open yourself up to what really matters and the things you truly love. You can have time for more fulfilling relationships, allow more space for new items, and you will appreciate the blessing of having all that you truly need. This, again, is not a one-and-done process, but throughout your whole life, you will need to take time to maintain and assess situations as seasons change and deal with things when it is time. I have close friends and family members who always laugh whenever I say with enthusiasm that I was piling up more stuff to get rid of. The typical response is asking me what in the world is there to get rid of because I hardly have much in the world in the first place. I simply reply that I will never cease finding something to get rid of because life is always revolving, and stuff constantly comes and goes.

Now, if you think that your family is just too big to downsize, simplifying and organizing is even more beneficial and necessary, and it is totally possible. When we had four young children, about every six months, I would go through their rooms to clear out broken toys and outgrown clothes. I knew what they still played with and what could be given away, and I would toss anything that needed to be thrown out. Simplifying is the first step in gaining some control over a large household and it will help with keeping your remaining stuff organized by having space for everything and a place to put it.

One area to be mindful of is our emotional attachments to things. You don't have to keep anything just because it has sentimental value. Sometimes, we hold onto things so tightly because of the memory attached to them, even though they serve no purpose whatsoever. When a loved one passes, you don't have to keep everything they owned. I chose to keep and cherish one or two of my favorite items or reminders when my grandmothers passed away, and they sit right out for me to see on a daily basis. The same rules apply to our wardrobes. Do you ever wonder why you have a closet full of clothes but can't ever find anything to wear? I worked for many years in office settings, so I had to dress professionally. I had a wide variety of tops, skirts and jewelry. Then, over a matter of time, I realized that I only wore my favorite outfits over and over. Everything else got shuffled to the back of the closet. We think we need so many options to pick from and that people will admire us more based on how we look, but in reality, nobody is really paying that much attention. And if they are, they love you more for who you are and not what you are wearing. At some point, I had to just get over myself. Now, I still wear pretty stuff, and I put in effort to look nice, but I don't need as many items to do so.

My greatest transition had to be the year that I literally got rid of almost everything I owned and decided to live out of my vehicle. I started that journey with more than I actually needed and found myself cutting back more and more within the first few months. My suitcase of clothes eventually dwindled down to a duffle bag, and I let go of two totes of belongings that I decided I did not want to hang onto anymore. I really wanted to know what it was like to be as simple and free as possible. I do not expect or recommend everybody to sell all that they own and become houseless unless it is a journey your heart desires as mine did. And if you have children still at home, there is a lot more to consider. However, I do know of many families that homeschool, live in a motorhome and travel around the country. I think that it is awesome that they are able to teach their children other important aspects of life that cannot be taught within the confines of a classroom.

As previously stated, this is not a poor mindset mentality because I am grateful to still have socks without holes in them and plenty of cute clothes to choose from. In fact, because I do not need much of anything, I can afford to splurge on having the few nice things that mean the most. I found that each season, I wear clothes that I feel the most comfortable in and look the best on me. So, every four to six months, as the weather changes, I can easily change my style as fashion trends change or my preferences. So, now I get to have a fresh, up-to-date look just by buying a few new things. Then, it's out with the old and in with the new. I wear the same flip-flops all summer long and the same boots all winter, and when they wear out, I just get a new pair. I have more time to have fun and be adventurous by keeping things so simple.

Another wardrobe secret of mine is that I love my black stretchy yoga pants (who doesn't), and because I basically wear them every day, I have a few of the same pair. This is one of the staples in my wardrobe. They are perfect and convenient for every occasion, whether I am just hanging around the house, going for a walk, going to church, going to a business meeting or going out on the town. All I have to do is change out the tops and the shoes, and I am ready for the next occasion. Do you know how quickly I can make a decision, get ready for anything and be out the door? I don't have a ton of options that keep me stuck in the cycle of what-should-I-wear or I-don't-have-anything-to-wear. It's another area of freedom when you can just revolve around the simplicity of what works best for you. Barack Obama's closet had the same color suits and ties to wear every day because he said he had to make enough big decisions being president that he didn't have time to decide what to wear.

All these principles can be applied to every part of your house: rooms, closets and drawers. One thing I will never, ever have in my home is a junk drawer because I do not keep junk. I consider it a highly organized drawer that contains miscellaneous items that I do need and use, which makes sense to me. Keeping things simple allows you to be more organized, which allows you to be more efficient with your time and schedule. It keeps your home and mind less susceptible to the clutter and chaos that the world so readily offers and helps make you feel like you have some control over your life. It is worth your time to make more time. And if you need help getting motivated or overwhelmed on where to start, there are professionals available to assist you in accomplishing your specific goals to create and maintain an orderly and functioning household for you and your family.

Life Lessons

- More stuff equals more clutter, which leads to more disorganization; less is more.

- Don't be afraid to take some risks or challenge yourself to let go of items that no longer serve a purpose. And if you find that you absolutely need it down the road, you can always get another one.

- Life is complicated enough, so keep it as simple as possible. You will never regret finding true freedom.

- Jesus tells us not to focus on storing up treasures on this earth, where moths and rust destroy them and which thieves can steal, but to store up our treasures in heaven, which will last for eternity.

- Technology and greed are abundantly growing and destroying our children and our relationships at an alarming rate, so bring your family back to a simpler place where love, respect and gratitude can flourish.

Prayer: *Lord, please remind us daily that the things of this world are temporary so that we would spend more time on that which has real eternal value instead. Amen.*

Declaration: *I am content in all circumstances, whether I am in need or have plenty (Philippians 4:11–12).*

CHAPTER 12

DEBT-FREE & SET FREE

"The steadfast love of the Lord never ceases"
(Lamentations 3:22, ESV).

Many of us as teenagers could not wait to grow up and have the freedom to be on our own, without anybody telling us what we could or could not do. However, most of us didn't realize the financial cost that came with that independence, such as rent, car payments, insurance, utilities and the ever-rising price of gas and groceries. Since our income is based on where we work, how often we work and how much we get paid, this determines how we live and what we can or can't afford. We eventually learn how to beg, borrow or steal to get what we want and need. The Bible says that the love of money is the root of all evil, and we all have some roots, right? Now, before we deem money as the enemy, we do need it to live and survive, at least a little bit. Without it, we would not be able to eat, have shelter, transportation, or basic household supplies. We even need money just to afford to die. I grew up hearing the classic line that the only two guarantees we have in life are death and taxes, and both of those cost money.

I started working as soon as I was old enough to get a job. I was about fifteen years old when I started cleaning tables at a local restaurant and eventually moved up to waitressing. This was the early '90s when a cup of coffee was only seventy-five cents. I had a lot of locals who met regularly for coffee every day after work, and they would just leave a dollar bill on the table, so I would get to keep the quarter as my tip. When I worked all day on a Saturday, I typically went home with forty dollars in quarters. I was finally at the age that I got my driver's license and wanted my own car. One of my regulars was selling an old 1985 Chevy Cavalier for $500. My parents didn't have a lot of extra money, so I knew I would have to come up with it on my own. Thankfully, my dad was a mechanic, so he would help me with the repairs needed to get it up and running.

I quickly saved up enough money to pay cash for it, plus my tags and insurance. I cleaned it up inside and out, put some new seat covers on, and it was all set to go. I am glad that while I was young, I had to work for the extra things that I wanted, so I learned to value and appreciate them rather than if they were just handed to me. I hope that some people in today's generation are being raised with the same work ethics we were back then. We are now, more than ever, in a society of play now and pay later. But the day to pay always comes, and usually with a higher price when we add all the interest from having to borrow.

Eventually, that car broke down past the point of repair, and I needed to get a new one. I fell in love with a 1988 Chevy Beretta with a five-speed manual stick shift. It had the power and pep I loved, and I had fun shifting it like a little hot rod. The only problem was that I didn't have the $1800 needed for it. This became my first experience borrowing money. My mom co-signed the loan for me, and I remember squealing the tires as I shifted from first to second gear out of the parking lot. I had a steady job, and it was a small loan that would only take about one and a half years to pay off.

I had established some credit so that the next car loan I got, I didn't even need a co-signer. It wasn't long before I established a pretty decent credit history, and the era of credit card power was in full effect. I remember one day running around the entire shopping mall, going to every department store that offered credit cards and I got approval from almost every single one. They sure were handy when I needed or wanted something that I couldn't afford to pay cash for at the moment. Of course, the only thing I didn't like was when the bill came the next month. I tried to pay off the balances each month to avoid interest, but that wasn't always possible.

At nineteen, I was already married, had a baby and rent

to pay, amongst other living expenses of being an adult. But, I worked hard and was responsible by paying my bills on time each month. My credit with debtors and people was important to me. My husband was establishing his credit, too. One day, he came home with a new computer that he had purchased with a loan. This was 1998, so the internet was just becoming prevalent, and I remember being so excited to order a pizza online. Eventually, he got a major credit card in the mail with a $5000 credit limit. I thought, who in their right mind would trust two young adults just starting out in life with that much credit? But we were keeping up with everything and looked like we were doing well for being so young. Although, I think that credit card was maxed out within the first week of getting it, and I have no idea what we even bought.

Unfortunately, within the following year, we went through our divorce. Now, here I was, a single mother having to hire a divorce lawyer and incur additional expenses, such as daycare. Then, I foolishly decided to buy an even more expensive car on a five-year loan only because I had the credit to do so. I was setting myself up for a downward spiral at some point, and eventually, it all caught up with me. I had remarried a few years later, bringing with me a mound of my own debt, as well as his huge amount of past due bills from a previous marriage. After paying as much back as we could over several years, we ended up combining what was left of our accumulated past-due balances and claimed Chapter 7 bankruptcy. This is not an easy decision, and the consequences should be carefully considered since it will remain on your credit history for up to ten years. However, I was grateful for the opportunity to have a fresh start and a second chance to make wiser financial decisions.

We had to surrender any secured debt, which included both of our cars, and find something cheap that we could pay with cash. With us now being debt-free, we were able to afford for me to stay home to raise our four children and live off only my husband's income. We stayed out of debt for many years after that, only using cash to buy anything we needed or wanted until we bought our first house. We were very intentional and responsible with our finances by not borrowing any more than we could comfortably afford to pay back. We did not apply for any credit cards for at least ten years, and any loans that we acquired were just for investing in house repairs. Over time, we were able to re-establish our credit, and our scores went back to excellent. The irony is that you need to borrow money to build good credit so that you have the credit to borrow more money. It just sounds like another vicious cycle to me.

Personally, I prefer to just have no debt at all. I absolutely love being debt-free. Unfortunately, with good credit and our impulsive human nature, we slowly got ourselves back into debt. We eventually bought two newer cars, got a few major credit cards and got sucked back into the "it feels good to get it now and pay later" cycle. One major credit card gave us a limit of $15,000. Again, who would trust us with that much credit? I got an attitude of entitlement and enjoyed the image of looking like we were on top again. We could have what we wanted when we wanted and deal with the consequences later. And just like my similar situation several years prior, shortly after accumulating all this debt, I went through another divorce.

I tried to hold it all together on my own, just like before. I paid as much back as I could, along with paying for another divorce attorney. It was only a matter of time before I had no choice but to file for Chapter 7 bankruptcy again. My excellent credit that I had worked so hard for went back down the drain. I am grateful that, yet again, I had the option to start over debt-free, even though it is something I wish I had never gone through. Especially twice in my life, but I learned that there is relief and life after bankruptcy.

I have found out on numerous occasions that paying in cash for a $2000–$3000 decent vehicle is my best investment. I can easily resell it when I am ready for something newer and use that money towards buying another vehicle, all while avoiding going into debt. Unlike buying a new car on a loan, which will eventually need repairs just like any other car, as well as payments. Plus, the value usually goes down as soon as you drive it off the lot. I know we put such an emphasis on how good we look based on what kind of car we drive, but really, we just need something reliable to get us to where we are going. And I can tell you from experience that pride will cost you much more than you bargained for. I have almost always been blessed with finding clean, reliable cars that are well-maintained and affordable; you just have to be willing to look.

Living a life that is free from debt is a choice and very possible. I have always found it better to have zero dollars than be negative and even better to be in the positive than at zero. I would rather be broke and not owe anyone than be in a position of having to pay someone back, along with interest. I believe it is an unnecessary stress that we could easily eliminate from our lives by choosing to live within our financial budgets. I know there are some debts that are unavoidable, such as buying a house, investing in a business or unexpected medical bills. But beyond that, we really don't need to borrow for much else. If you do, just be cautious not to stretch it further than you absolutely have to. Eventually, any structure will collapse when too much pressure is applied, and the same goes for your budget.

- Living debt-free in today's society is absolutely possible and totally worth the freedom and peace of mind from abstaining from substantial debt.
- Proverbs 22:7 tells us that the debtor is a slave to the lender, so we can choose to set ourselves free.
- One of the most common things couples fight over is money, so eliminating unnecessary spending and living within your budget will help your marriage have one less thing to stress about.
- If you are facing overwhelming debt, there is help available. Seek a financial advisor or resource, such as a Dave Ramsey course, to get out of debt and live the abundant life that God desires for you.

Prayer: *Lord, I pray that anyone struggling with debt will find creative or miraculous ways to pay it off and show us how we can be wise stewards with all that You have given us. Amen.*

Declaration: *God provides all of my needs according to His riches in glory by Christ Jesus (Philippians 4:19).*

CHAPTER 13

THERE'S A FUNGUS AMONG US

"But the fruit of the Spirit is love"
(Galatians 5:22, NKJV).

I have struggled with my weight and food addiction most of my life, as far back as the fifth grade. At that time, my brother and I lived with my dad and grandmother for the school year. Neither one of my parents had much money, so we grew up with the assistance of welfare. I still hear about how amazing the government cheese was, but I was too young to remember. However, I do remember how much I loved my dad's spaghetti. I have always loved pasta...and pizza...and cereal...and chocolate...anything full of carbs and sugar. Then, when I hit my teenage years, I had to pretty much starve myself just to stay slim. And when I got pregnant at eighteen, I had gained seventy-five pounds by the time I gave birth to my daughter. My all-or-nothing thinking even applied to my relationship with food, so I was either binge eating due to my emotions or starving myself as a form of punishment for overeating.

The first time I ever heard about Candida was in my late twenties. I was in the middle of my battle with severe anxiety when a friend introduced me to this mysterious word. Candida, or Candida albicans, is a yeast-like fungus that lives within the human gastrointestinal tract. Nowadays, you hear much more often about the importance of our gut health or leaky gut syndrome, and this is what they are basically referring to. We all have some yeast throughout our bodies, but the good bacteria can usually keep it under control unless you allow it to overproduce. This fungus lives, thrives and excessively multiplies by feeding mostly on sugar or things that can raise your blood sugar, such as alcohol or excess stress, as well as the use of antibiotics. With today's all-American diet, we can see why this issue has become so prevalent, and obesity in our nation continues to grow significantly. So, how do you know if you have an issue with the overgrowth of yeast? Here is a list of the most common symptoms associated with Candida found in our gut:

- Frequent or intense sugar cravings
- Food allergies
- Finger or toenail infections
- Athlete's foot
- Ringworm
- Recurring yeast infections (in women)
- Constipation, bloating or gas
- Irritable bowel syndrome

- Joint pain
- Muscle tension and aches
- Mucus buildup
- Weakened immune system
- Obesity
- Shortness of breath
- Chronic fatigue
- Poor memory
- Lack of concentration
- Mood swings and irritability
- Depression or anxiety

Of course, there are many other factors that can cause some of the symptoms listed above, but an overabundance of sugar in your diet could be a huge culprit. I have struggled with many of these symptoms for much of my life. I was obese from eating a lot of processed and sugary foods and constantly dealt with fungal infections, along with frequent constipation and gas. Plus, I dealt with fatigue, irritability, anxiety and what is known as a foggy brain most of my days. Now, finding out what the cause of many of my issues was much easier than actually fixing them. I don't have to tell you how much we all probably struggle with our diet, but cutting sugar out seemed nearly impossible. Besides, the immediate side effects of sugar withdrawal are like coming off almost any other drug or substance. Sugar addiction is real.

If you consume a lot of carbohydrates or processed foods on a regular basis, completely eliminating them can cause your body to experience some severe withdrawal symptoms. Some of them may include anxiety, increased sugar cravings, headaches, body chills, cold sweats and other flu-like symptoms. However, this is just temporary as your body detoxes from all the excess sugar. This is known as the die-off stage, which is when the fungus is now being starved to death. It is important to know that you do not starve yourself but the food source that causes the yeast to survive. Like any addiction, the unpleasant withdrawal symptoms and extreme cravings experienced while detoxing can easily cause you to go back for another sugar fix. The good news is that any sick feelings typically only last the first few days, and then you start to feel better, maybe much better, as your body is actually healing and gaining more energy.

When I finally got sick and tired of being sick and tired, I decided to tackle my health issues. I wanted to feel better physically, mentally and emotionally, so I looked further into the anti-Candida diet. The only way to kill off the excess yeast in my gut was to eat primarily protein, healthy fats and low-carb fruits and vegetables. Within three days of eliminating sugary and processed foods from my diet, I started noticing that my body was healing, and I had never felt so good in my life. My neck and shoulders had no tension, and my knees didn't crackle when walking up and down the stairs. I could breathe easier when doing regular movement and even had the energy and desire to run, which I would not do unless someone was chasing me. I was so aware and alert that my mind had complete clarity. I had absolutely no anxiety and could not cause myself to go into a panic attack even if I tried to push the limits of my thoughts. The excess fat started melting off instantly, and I lost twenty pounds in the first two weeks without adding any exercise. Again, I did not starve myself at all because I love food and need it to function throughout the day. In fact, the simplicity of this meal plan is that you can eat as much of the recommended foods as you want, whenever you want and without restricting calories.

Now, if you are very determined, you can try to use just your willpower to get through the first few days of detoxing without wanting to relapse, but another option is taking a high-quality enzyme to help avoid the symptoms of die-off, along with a probiotic to rebuild your healthy gut bacteria. Now, I have never followed popular diets like Atkins (which is high protein/low carb meal plans) or the Keto diet (which is high fat/low carb meal plans), but you can see that people do get results by lowering their carb and sugar intake because your body goes into a state of ketosis where it uses stored fat to fuel its energy instead of glucose, turning your body into a fat burning machine.

Another point I try to make is that I no longer like to use the words diet and exercise because these have been turned into an idea of restricted or excessive ways to lose weight. Now, you may say, but wait, you are talking about a restrictive diet. However, I am actually promoting making better lifestyle choices that become your new way of living a longer, more vibrant and fulfilling life. The actual word diet just refers to whatever it is that we eat, so we can change our diet without going on a diet. The goal is to create a more intentional meal plan by replacing junk food with real, whole food to create and sustain a healthier body.

Below, I listed some of the ideal foods to assist in your fight against Candida overgrowth.

Meat
(All-Natural without Added Hormones or Antibiotics)
- Chicken
- Beef
- Fish
- Venison

- Eggs

Vegetables (Non-Starchy)
- Lettuce (any kind of leafy greens)
- Broccoli
- Cauliflower
- Celery
- Cabbage
- Brussel sprouts
- Cucumber
- Onions
- Spinach
- Tomatoes
- Zucchini

Fruits (Low-Sugar)
- Strawberries
- Blueberries
- Raspberries
- Blackberries
- Lemons and limes

Nuts & Seeds (Low-Mold)
- Almonds
- Hazelnuts
- Coconut

- Flaxseed
- Sunflower seeds

Healthy Fats & Oils

- Avocado
- Extra virgin olive oil—cold compressed
- Coconut oil
- Flax oil
- Sesame oil

Once you have the Candida under control, you can start adding more natural fruits and healthy grains back into your meals. In 2018, I had the opportunity to stay with my friend, a nutritionist, as mentioned in a previous chapter, for a couple of weeks because I wanted to tackle my health issues and obesity again. I had let it slip out of control and was at my highest weight ever, 240 pounds, even more than the day I gave birth to my daughter. My friend and other relatives I spent much time with while living out of my minivan did not eat meat, so my diet consisted of much more plant-based foods. This was ideal as I was pretty nomadic most of the time and did not have access to a refrigerator or way of cooking food very often. Traveling around with mostly fruits, vegetables, nuts and seeds was very convenient for this lifestyle. Plus, I had a lot of health improvements just by cutting out the refined sugars and processed foods again, and within three days, any inflammation in my joints and bones went way down, the excess weight started falling off, and I was twenty-five pounds lighter within the first month.

I have found through research and many different opinions that the great debate seems to be whether to eat meat or not. I love what the apostle Paul says in Romans 14 that if you believe you should eat meat, eat meat; if you don't, then don't. Of course, he writes a lot more in-depth on this, and the importance of the point he is trying to make is not to judge each other based on these differences but, in faith, to do what you are called to do. But there is no doubt that the best thing we can do within our own diets is to cut out the excess refined sugars, bread, pasta, and processed foods that are known to be high in preservatives and sodium, which are so prevalent in our society. A good habit to incorporate is shopping the outer aisles of the grocery store since most of your produce and whole foods will be found there. Also, read the labels to see what ingredients are in the foods you purchase. Whole or natural foods will only have a few simple ingredients listed, and you will actually be able to pronounce them. Another rule of thumb when it comes to fruits and vegetables is fresh is best and frozen is good, but try to stay away from canned foods as they are typically saturated in heavy syrups or salt.

It's best to fill your plate with whole foods containing a balance of healthy proteins, fats and complex carbs, such as fruits, vegetables and whole grains. If you don't eat fish, flaxseed is the highest-containing plant-based source of Omega 3, which is great for your brain health and easy to add to your meals or smoothies. Every food is categorized into one of three macronutrients: protein, fat or carbohydrate. Even if a food has some grams of each, the highest listed number is the macro that food will fit into. For example, peanut butter has 17g of fat, 8g of protein and 7g of carbs, so it would be considered as a fat product since the highest gram listed is fat.

We should try to balance our macros on a daily basis and not completely eliminate one or the other since they are all necessary components for our health. The only thing to stay clear from or as minimally as possible is simple carbs versus complex carbs. Our carb intake should come primarily from fruits and vegetables, which our body is designed to absorb without drastically spiking our blood sugar, and they contain several micronutrients and vitamins that our body needs. Unlike simple carbs that contain white sugar, white flour and white pasta, which cause our blood sugar to instantly rise and then eventually drop. Balancing our healthy and whole foods helps keep our blood sugar and mind stabilized throughout the day to allow us to perform at optimal level.

Water is another key component to sustaining a healthy life and is essentially vital for the proper function of our body, brain and intestinal health. Our bodies are made up of almost 60 percent water, and our brains are about 73 percent. Even the earth itself is over 70 percent water. Needless to say, God created water to be a crucial part of our life source, and we would not survive very long without it. Many experts agree that we should drink about half of our weight in ounces of clean, filtered water. For example, if you weigh 150 pounds, that would equal around seventy-five ounces of water per day. The best way to start your day is to begin hydrating immediately. I now have the habit of drinking twenty to forty ounces of water within the first hour of getting up and before eating anything else. It is a great way to tell your body and your mind that it is time to wake up and get moving. That may sound like a lot of water, but once you start drinking more of it, your body will be refreshed and actually start craving it. If you don't like the taste of plain water, throw a lemon or lime in it for flavor and added antioxidants.

Other changes I made over the years were to replace dairy milk with almond milk, sugary cereal with whole grain cereal, white bread with multi-grain bread, margarine with real butter, vegetable oil with olive or coconut oil, iodized salt with sea salt and canned fruits and vegetables with fresh or frozen. I eliminated anything that had high fructose corn syrup, hydrogenated oils and other harmful ingredients. In fact, I don't try to buy anything that has more than just a few simple ingredients. I look for peanut butter that just says peanuts or brown rice noodles that just say brown rice. My kids were quite little when I started learning all these things about health and began to take it seriously, so they hated going grocery shopping with me because I would stop to read the labels of every single thing before I bought it. But, over time, your new habits become easier and normal.

If you have a busy schedule like me, it is so easy just to swing into a fast-food restaurant and grab that so-tasty, greasy cheeseburger, salty fries and large soda pop. But, honestly, it makes me extremely tired, and I feel horrible before I even finish my meal, so I just don't find it as tempting anymore. Once you start feeling better, you don't want to go back to feeling that bad. Even your taste buds will change so that the sweet and salty things you used to love won't be as enjoyable. And to be clear, this is not just about looking better but feeling better by having more energy, more self-confidence and less excess weight to carry around. They say if you fail to plan, then plan to fail, so it is important that you stock up on healthy foods and snacks to be readily available in your bag, purse or car for when you do get hungry.

I often hear people say, and I used to agree, that it is so much more expensive to eat healthy, but I can tell you that is not true. A fast-food meal now ranges from seven to ten dollars, with prices steadily increasing. For that price, I can grab enough lettuce, fruit and vegetables to make three to five huge salads. I can grab a week's worth of apples for less than one meal at a restaurant. A cost-efficient way to purchase fresh produce is to buy foods that are currently in season, as they are typically cheaper or even on sale. You do not have to buy everything organic or go to an expensive health food store unless there is something specific you prefer. One key to making this a successful transition is to not buy any junk food or unhealthy snacks because you will be tempted to eat that instead of the healthy foods you purchased, then they will just end up spoiling, and you're wasting money. Now, you may think that salad and apples won't fill you up, but that is primarily because your body may be currently used to consuming 1000–1500 calories in one meal, which is about what our entire daily intake should be. No wonder the battle of the bulge has truly become a battle, but it is one that we can win with proper nutrition and lifestyle choices.

Give your body a few days to see how quickly it can adjust and enjoy new foods, and allow your palate to change from what it used to like to what it really desires. You will naturally start to crave more real food and fresh water, and your body will thank you. It is also fun experimenting and creating so many different recipes with healthy, whole foods. The possibilities are endless, and so are the flavors. Plus, how much are you willing to sell your health for? Diabetes and cancer treatment cost more money than eating healthy ever will, and who can put a price on the possibility of a longer life? Now, I write from my own personal journey of discovering how to be healthy over the past couple of decades and what I have experienced or been taught. I don't have it all perfect and still struggle to find the right balance for myself at times. And there are always variances in what even the professionals believe, trust me, as I have worked closely with many of them.

I just want you to know how simple, affordable, and life-changing eating healthier can be. If you have a very fast-paced lifestyle and not much time for cooking, you can easily make a smoothie or salad and grab some fresh fruit on the go. If you have more time or like cooking, you can whip up a veggie omelet for breakfast or chicken and veggie stir fry for dinner. Some other healthier food replacement ideas are mashed cauliflower instead of potatoes, brown rice or spiraled zucchini noodles instead of white pasta or homemade veggie pizza on a thin whole-grain crust topped with all-natural marinara sauce and healthy meats and vegetables. For dessert ideas, dark chocolate (70 percent cocoa) instead of milk chocolate, fruit smoothie or frozen yogurt instead of ice cream, or a yogurt parfait. I have been able to make some of my favorite meals but with healthier ingredients so that I can enjoy them without the consequences of feeling bad physically, mentally or emotionally. And with Google at your fingertips, you can access countless recipes.

Life Lessons

- God created our bodies and the foods to properly fuel them. Most of the food we are now accustomed to is not even real food at all and full of unhealthy preservatives and chemicals.
- We don't have to live in deprivation to be disciplined and can actually enjoy the blessings of healthy foods more abundantly.
- Ecclesiastes says that there is a time and season for everything under heaven, and this could include fasting and feasting. Prayerfully ask God what is best for the health of you and your family at this time.
- The right foods are life-giving and will bring forth a healthier, happier life. You can love them, too.

Prayer: *Lord, we thank You that You created our bodies to live and thrive in this world, and we ask You to help us live responsibly to take care of them. Amen.*

Declaration: *Whether I eat or drink or whatever I do, I do it all for the glory of God (1 Corinthians 10:31).*

CHAPTER 14

MENTAL ILLNESS–A STATE OF MIND?

"My peace I give to you" (John 14:27, NKJV).

The most significant and crucial area of my life that I have struggled extensively and most detrimentally was my own mental health. As complex and controversial as the subject of mental illness is, I am up for the challenge to uncover many truths that I have discovered in my life over the past forty years. I am not a licensed professional, and the information I disclose is merely from my own experiences, opinions and extensive research. If you are truly struggling with severe mental health issues or feel like hurting yourself or somebody else, please seek professional help immediately. It could save your life and prevent the heartache of your loved ones.

You would have to live under a rock not to be aware of the pharmaceutical companies advertising their next manufactured solution trying to help people find happiness or, at minimum, cope with their anxiety and depression. Of course, the great controversy is whether this is really helping or if they are just building a multi-billion-dollar industry. First and foremost, I want to remove any stigma linked to the use of medication for severe mental health issues because it would be no different than taking medication for any physical ailments we may suffer. Regardless, most medications are unable to cure diseases but only alleviate the symptoms. Unfortunately, the risk with these medications is that they have as many or even worse side effects than the issues we are trying to overcome. So I ask, is there another way? Is there a better way?

Another question to consider: are the medical professional's examinations of each patient comprehensive enough to accurately diagnose whether the issue is coming from an actual chemical imbalance, or are they merely diagnosing behaviors without confirming the cause? When I struggled over the years with what many would consider manic-depressive behavior, bouncing from extreme depression, anxiety and thoughts of suicide to extreme happiness, excitement and mania, a therapist simply diagnosed me after a five-minute consultation without any further examination. She basically gave me a prescription and wished me luck as she sent me out the door. Well, my primary doctor did suggest therapy. I was warned that the pills for my mood swings and anxiety might intensify the scary thoughts and emotions that I was already enduring, so I was too scared to even take them. These few options did not give me much hope or real answers on how to get well. What I have learned along my journey to acquire peace and sanity I am going to share with you, and I hope this good news will help bring you hope and healing as well.

I was pretty young when I started having suicidal thoughts, maybe before I was even a teenager, but I am not quite sure. Being a perfectionist from basically birth and struggling with an all-or-nothing mindset led me to see everything as merely black or white. I didn't have any balance to keep my emotions stabilized. I was also a very deep thinker, analyzing everything to death, which left me worrying constantly. I was very sensitive to people and energy around me, and I could feel everything in every situation very deeply. My way of thinking and my perceptions of life caused me to live in a state of deep darkness, anxiety and confusion most of the time, even though I was really good at looking happy. I had so many issues and believed the odds were really stacked against me. Mental illness runs rampant on my mother's side of the family, especially depression and codependency issues. Then, major sexual dysfunctions and perversions of incest ran deep on my dad's side, so I jokingly say how my mother and father met, bred and had my brother and me. I seriously thought I was a hopeless cause and that there would be no way for me to live a life free from mental illness. Thank God I was wrong, and He showed me the way out. However, a word of caution: this was not an overnight process, and it took years of hard work and dedication to fight for my freedom. But I promise, it is possible and so worth it.

One thing I discovered is that many of the Bible's most prominent people also struggled with the same mental health issues we face today, so it is nothing new. Yet, we seem shocked when we ourselves or someone we know fall into the deep pit of depression, anxiety, or struggle with thoughts of doom and gloom. The day after Elijah's victory of defeating 850 false prophets, he sat under a broom tree praying for God to let him die. Have you ever wanted God to just take your life? I know I have. But instead, God sent an angel to give him food, and Elijah ate and slept. Sometimes, we just need a break. And sometimes, the answer isn't that simple. I am thankful that we have come a long way in understanding and properly treating these kinds of issues, mostly over just the past few decades. It was not long ago that professionals did not know how to handle patients suffering from mental disabilities, so they were just considered insane and locked away in an asylum or mental hospital to protect society from them and them from themselves. If that were still the case today, many of us would probably be in a padded room right now. I know I probably would.

Another interesting thing I learned was that there are over a hundred causes of depression and anxiety. But the good news is that there are over a hundred remedies, as well. I am not going to address them all, but I do want to highlight some of the major causes and solutions that many of us deal with and which ones helped me the most. One thing I had to get over was the cliché that, as a Christian, I should not have any issues with anxiety or depression. If we have Jesus, we should be the happiest people on Earth, right? Simplistically, yes, but in reality, it's not that easy. I believed or was told that I was lacking in my faith and was not trusting Jesus or suffering from the sin in my life. Although, as well-intentioned as these people were regarding faith, there seemed to be a lack of awareness that we still live in the flesh, a broken world and probably come from a broken family. And it takes time to heal and grow in our faith in God.

In fact, the expectations I allowed other people and the church to put on me only negatively impacted and hindered my recovery from depression and anxiety because I feared even more about not being perfect. I strived so hard not to let anybody down that it made me physically and mentally sick. My viewpoint of people reflected my perception of God as well, so I lived in fear that He was mad at me for being imperfect, too. But now I know that God loves me just the way He created me, even with my flaws and weaknesses, and the same goes for you. He is not mad at us and actually rejoices over us with singing. I mean, what parent who truly loves their children would despise them in the midst of their pain and suffering? In Psalms 34:18, we are told that God is close to the brokenhearted and saves those who are crushed in spirit. So, we have this hope to cling to: God is near, and He will save us. This true faith became the foundation on which I was able to build everything else: that God loves me, hears me, saves me and is faithful to keep His promises.

As stated in a previous chapter, we are a three-part being, so it is important that we address and learn to take care of ourselves in all three areas—physically, mentally and spiritually. So, let's start with our physical body, which was created as a living organism and requires specific components to thrive at its peak performance. Whatever we put in our bodies directly affects every aspect of our body, including our brain, whether it be good or bad. Our bodies were meant to be fueled by real, whole foods that give us the important vitamins and nutrients that it needs to function properly. It would be like putting sand in your gas tank and expecting it to still run. It just won't run as well or eventually break down.

Other than proper food and plenty of water, we also

need an abundance of fresh air, movement and sunlight, to name a few other remedies that can tremendously help alleviate the symptoms of depression and anxiety. This is why seasonal affective disorder (SAD) is so common, especially during the winter months, because of the lack of daylight and being cooped up inside for several months. I struggled with this as well until I found a few things that helped me to get through the long, dark winter seasons we have here in Michigan. I now stay active by going to the gym for exercise, doing laps at an indoor swimming pool and staying social with friends and family. It also helps to know that the winter equinox is on December 21, which is the shortest day of the year, so we can look forward to gaining a little daylight each day after this point. It helps our perspective to know that there is light at the end of the tunnel. Speaking of light, you can also incorporate light therapy or a blue light box to help enhance your mood.

Our minds are very complex, with over 100 billion neurons continually sending and retrieving information using electrochemical signals. Then, there are seven neurotransmitters, which include serotonin, dopamine and endorphins. Therefore, there is no reason not to believe that we cannot have some misfires, which would be known as a chemical imbalance. However, the majority of depression and anxiety cases are not merely due to chemical imbalances, and that is being proven with the advancement of psychology. We know that genetics may play a role, but that is only one factor that can still be overcome by learning new techniques and perspectives, which can actually rewire the limbic system of your brain. This is powerful information!

And because I was told genetics was a cause of mental health issues, I believed it was something I could not fix because it wasn't something I could change. My mom and one of her sisters even had to undergo electroshock therapy (ECT) several times when they were younger. For those who do not know, this procedure consists of sending small currents of electricity through the brain to change its chemistry and is supposed to reverse the symptoms of depression and anxiety. I think of it like a computer that has gone on the fritz, and you need to push the reset button to get it to function properly again. I was around ten years old when my mom was admitted to the psychiatric hospital after she told some family members that she thought it would be best if she took her own life and even thought of taking me and my brother with her. She felt so much pain and sorrow that her distorted thoughts made her believe that we would all be better off if we just went to heaven. In her mind, she probably didn't think of it as hurting us but saving us from the pain of this world. The first session my mom had seemed to have helped bring her out of that dark place, although they gave her three more treatments just to make sure. After a few months' stay, she finally got to come home and was never hospitalized for that length of time again.

Now, the frontal lobe of the brain, which is the largest of the four major lobes, is responsible for our memories, emotions, decision-making skills and conscience. This is where our cognitive behavioral skills are developed. I think my thoughts, more than anything else, were and are the leading cause of most of my bouts of depression and anxiety. I used to wonder how this could be because I was not choosing to feel sad or hopeless, but I couldn't get myself to just think happy thoughts. Well, it is deeper than that, and it takes a while to replace all the distorted thoughts and lies that we believe about ourselves or our situations with the truth. The hardest part is not even knowing the truth but actually believing it. Somebody could tell me that I was valuable or special over and over, but until I accepted it as the truth for myself, they were only words.

According to the Diagnostic and Statistical Manual of Mental Disorders, 5th Edition (DSM-5), there are currently ten different types of personality disorders, which are forms of mental illness. They are grouped into three clusters, with some of them having similar traits or overlapping each other. Much like any other mental illness, these disorders range on a spectrum of severity, depending on each individual person and their circumstances. The more severe the personality disorder is, the more erratic or dysfunctional the person acts. People with any type of mental illness, including personality disorders, could still benefit by applying these techniques, such as cognitive behavioral therapy, a healthy diet, exercise, as well as avoiding drug or alcohol use. And, if you are in a close relationship with someone suffering from one of these disorders and they refuse to get help or treatment, you could find yourself in a very toxic or abusive relationship. You may need to set firm boundaries or even go no-contact to prevent yourself from enabling their behavior or possibly being put in a dangerous situation. In fact, one of the biggest ways I was able to flourish in my own mental health recovery was by removing myself from several toxic or abusive relationships that were destroying my self-worth.

Let me also remind you that seasons of depression and anxiety can be the result of specific situations. Most likely, at some point in your life, you will endure some kind of loss, death or heartbreak. Even though we do not like to feel pain and try to avoid it at all costs, it is not always going to be possible. And if we did not have emotions and feelings triggered by loss, we would almost be inhumane or sociopathic. Allowing yourself the time needed to go through the grieving process is necessary for healing. I know that people try to offer us a quick fix or sugarcoat our disappointments with fancy words or scriptures, but crying is a very natural and necessary part of releasing pain. Give yourself the grace and self-care that you need while enduring traumatic experiences and losses. God is your healer, and you will make it through. Let time mend your heart, but don't get stuck in the process. One of my greatest reminders is that everything in this life is temporary, and this, too, shall pass. Life is short, and only eternity lasts forever, which is what matters most. It is this hope we can cling to while we go through the challenges and hard times in our life.

Once I started getting my thinking right, changing my lifestyle choices and eliminating toxic relationships, my confidence grew, and I continued further along my healing journey. These significant truths became my new standards, and I was able to create a better life for myself and those around me. I realized there are two ways to process thoughts and the outcomes that follow:

Negative thoughts = negative feelings = negative words = negative behavior = negative results.

Positive thoughts = positive feelings = positive words
= positive behavior = positive results.

I am ever so grateful that I survived the many dark years that I struggled with suicidal thoughts, and I mean survived. Unfortunately, many have not, and that breaks my heart. So many people are missing loved ones because they chose to take their own life. Years ago, I prayed to God not to ever let me take my own life, and now I am so thankful that I was around to experience so many good days that I would have missed otherwise. There are better days ahead, and you can and will enjoy life again. You never know what God has in store for you tomorrow. I learned that just because I have one bad day doesn't mean I am destined to have all bad days. Brighter days will come for you, just as they did for me, if you hang on and fight the good fight of faith. You are loved, you are important, you have a purpose.

Life Lessons

- The battle for our own mental health is truly one of our greatest challenges to conquer, but it can be won if we do not give up.
- God created you on purpose and for a specific purpose. Most importantly, to be in fellowship with

Him, so seek Him in all that you do so that you can grow in your faith.

- The stigma of mental health has been broken over the past several years, so there is no shame in sharing your struggles and asking for help, for every person also goes through these things at some point in their life.
- If you are having thoughts of suicide or self-harm, please find someone safe to talk to or seek professional counseling. There is help available, and your life is worth saving.

Prayer: *Lord, I pray that all who are suffering from the anguish of mental illness would be filled with Your peace that surpasses all understanding. Amen.*

Declaration: *I am not anxious about anything but pray over every situation with thanksgiving, and the peace of God will guard my heart and mind (Philippians 4:6–7).*

CHAPTER 15

FAITH VS. FEAR

"With His love, he will calm all your fears"
(Zephaniah 3:17, NLT).

We don't have to look very far into our own lives to see why fear is mentioned over 365 times in the Bible. It's basically a needed reminder for every day of the year. I believe fear is the root cause of every issue in life; yes, every single one. We can evaluate just how much fear controls and governs our life and those around us with just a few examples. We may strive for perfection due to the fear of not being accepted or approved. People with control issues use manipulative tactics for fear of losing control. Greed and selfishness come from the fear of not having enough. Revenge is based on the fear of not receiving justice for an offense. Pride is stemmed from the insecurity of not being good enough. And rebellion is caused by the fear of not getting what we want. The list goes on and on, so I can see why God has to make this such an important subject in the Bible. Fear is His greatest contender and the most powerful tool used by the devil.

We can see how the pandemic of 2020 instilled fears

all around the world and stopped us completely in our tracks. If you were alive during this timeframe as well, I really don't have to go into much detail on the mass chaos and panic it caused. The fears were too many to count and affected everybody. Some of the fears were rational, and some seemed irrational. I saw the extreme fear result from one group of people who believed they were losing their freedom and rights and another group who severely feared getting sick or dying. The public media, as well as underground sources, were also playing their part to feed these fears. We heard so many theories and conspiracies from every side, which made it almost impossible to know what was true or what was false. Either way, fear abounded and spread like wildfire. Now, I am not going to take any side or downplay the extent of what happened. People lost their lives, lost loved ones, lost homes, lost jobs, lost businesses and some lost their minds. In the beginning, I even succumbed to paralyzing fear until I decided that I would rather die than go back to the prison of fear. So I turned off the media, turned off the noise, grabbed my kayak and went to the only place I knew that offered serenity and sanity, out in the quiet beauty of nature.

Eventually, I did end up contracting COVID-19 and was quarantined for fourteen days. I was scared but chose to stand in faith each day, knowing that God was ultimately in control if I lived or died. I prayed for life but merely put the outcome in His hands. Thankfully, my case was mild, and since I was in time out anyway for two weeks, I took the opportunity to read fourteen books of the New Testament in the Bible. I understand that many were not as fortunate, and my heart goes out to everyone who suffered through this time and lost loved ones. We are constantly reminded that we only have two options when faced with any scenario in life: faith or fear, and I have experienced both in my own life.

Now, everybody struggles with fear now and then; it's human nature, but some may be more prone to it due to life experiences and past traumas. I am sure my drive for perfectionism, being a people pleaser and having a long history of abuse and rejection had quite an impact on my life. I was an avid worrier; it was my daily companion for much of my life, and I still face opportunities where I have to stand against fear today. I remember a time when I used to worry so much that if I wasn't worrying, I would worry because I knew there had to be something to worry about. Even though I had deep, nagging fears on the one hand, I was kind of a daredevil and rebellious on the other. I loved flying, riding rollercoasters and traveling. I was not at all scared of heights. I did anything for a thrill, as it made me feel alive. I grew up watching every scary movie that came out. I was a big fan of the typical '80s horror flicks, such as *Nightmare on Elm Street, Friday the 13th,* and *Halloween,* to name a few.

It wasn't until 2005 that I had my first panic attack. I was driving a friend and my children to church one Sunday when my mind and body just went into another dimension of fear and sheer terror. It was one of the scariest feelings I ever had in my life. I sat during the entire service thinking I was going crazy or going to die, and I couldn't tell anyone; I was too scared to even speak. This would be the first of many panic attacks. It came out of the blue, and I have no idea what triggered it; maybe everything just caught up with me at once. Surprisingly, it was actually after a lot of the chaos and drama stopped in my life, but just because it physically stopped didn't mean it automatically stopped in my mind. It's like when a massive hurricane hits and causes all sorts of destruction, but once it passes, then all of the damage has to be dealt with. My external life had finally quieted when the fear abruptly came crashing within. In fact, sometimes, we unknowingly use drama to drown out the voices inside our heads. I was finally finding peace in my heart and getting closer to God; only I didn't know this was just a start of a whole new journey of healing.

These panic attacks started coming more frequently, at random times and occasions, with no warning or apparent reason. It would happen when I was driving, standing in line at the grocery store or at church; really anywhere and at any time. At first, I thought this was merely a spiritual attack. I had been recently learning about my identity and authority in Jesus Christ through the teachings of Freedom in Christ Ministries by Neil T. Anderson. I used powerful prayers found in his books and constantly rebuked the devil. Sometimes that worked, sometimes it didn't. Over time, the panic attacks didn't go away but actually got more severe. Sometimes, I was rushed to the hospital for fear of having a heart attack or thinking I was going to pass out. One time, I had to have my husband pick me up from the grocery store because I could not drive home. Over time, any place where I had experienced a panic attack, I would then try to avoid that in the future, if at all possible. I stopped driving on highways, traveling too far from home or almost anything that consisted of leaving the house. At this point, I had become very much agoraphobic, which is a debilitating anxiety condition of living in constant fear while away from home. Even though it seemed irrational, I couldn't figure out how to fix it, especially when I didn't know what was causing it.

I was too scared to be alone. It got to the point that when my husband would leave for work every morning while it was still dark outside, I would lay in my bed, paralyzed with fear. After lying in bed without being able to move or speak for more than an hour, I finally mustered up the only little bit of courage I could and say the name of Jesus out loud. Immediately, whatever dark presence I felt holding me down would leave. Morning after morning, this happened. Eventually, I spoke the name of Jesus out loud after only forty-five minutes. Then, I would say His name within thirty minutes until I finally had the courage to start saying His name as soon as I felt the presence of fear. After some time, the devil knew he had lost his power in that situation and left me alone.

Since I had recently learned the reality and magnitude of spiritual warfare, I spent much of my days casting out demons and rebuking the devil. Even though it was important to learn about the very real impact of the spiritual realm, God finally spoke to me one day in my spirit and told me that I was basically having an illicit affair on Him. In my astonishment, I asked what He meant by that. And He replied that I spent most of my time fighting with the devil rather than spending my time with Him. I saw it so clearly, and my heart was instantly broken and convicted. God wanted to spend time with me, but I was too busy spending it yelling at the devil.

To be clear, there is nothing wrong with using our authority to cast out demonic powers, but I had gone to the extreme where that was all I was doing. His truth set me free at that moment as I could now experience a relationship with God instead of all the demons. James 4:7 (NKJV) says, "Therefore submit to God. Resist the devil and he will flee from you." I oftentimes hear sermons preached where they just say to resist the devil and he will flee, but they miss the most important part of this command about submitting to the Lord first. When we are in the presence of God, the devil flees.

Even with this new revelation, I continued to struggle with panic attacks. I still had so much healing to go through due to my past traumas, which took many more years of learning and discovery. I found out that even though you feel like you are going to faint, die or go crazy, you are not. I learned that most of my panic attacks were caused by my own thoughts and that I had the capability to change them if I didn't like what was playing in my mind. I made huge progress when I stopped following the scary thoughts down the rabbit trail to see how far they would go because I realized they never lead anywhere good. I also learned that certain chemicals in your body cause anxiety, especially sugar, caffeine and nicotine, so I cut as much of that out as possible.

Another major factor, again, was toxic and abusive relationships. I don't blame other people for my issues because I am responsible for my own healing journey and boundaries. But being around negative or critical personalities does not help you thrive at your best and can hinder your personal growth. Trying to live up to the expectations of those who regularly criticize or demean you will only bring you further down, especially when they intentionally know how to push your buttons and try to control you with fear. I realized that fear is like a snake. It coils around you as they do to their prey, and every time you exhale, it tightens its grip until it restricts your breathing. The more we give into fear, the more power it gains. Franklin Roosevelt was absolutely correct when he said that there is nothing to fear but fear itself. As long as you allow the feelings of fear to stop you, you won't get very far.

I finally got to a point where I had enough. I realized the only way to overcome all of my fears was to face them, each one at a time. I no longer wanted to live this way, so I was willing to step out of the boat in order to get to the other side. I figured it had to be better than living like this. Part of my problem was that, as a very sensitive person who feels everything deeply, it causes me to overthink and analyze every detail. I couldn't even look up at the clouds without having a panic attack because I would see how vast and limitless the sky was, and it would frighten me. My mind was easily overwhelmed and terrified by the most insignificant thoughts.

But I had to learn how to come up for air, completely change how I observed and perceived things and stop dramatizing every single thought. In one of the books I read called *Panic Away* by Barry McDonagh, I found a technique that I could use whenever I started to get the sensations of anxiety, and my brain was going into fight or flight mode. I was able to sit somewhere quiet and alone for just a few minutes, close my eyes and make my mind induce the panic to its heightened extent. Once it peaked, it would quickly subside. This was an amazing discovery in helping me not only stop the panic attacks but learn not to fear them. If I could take my power back, then the less often the attacks would happen. Fear loses its power when you are no longer afraid of it because you just took its primary weapon away, which is fear itself.

I think one of the greatest fears I've had since childhood was the fear of dying. It's something we will all have to face (unless Jesus returns beforehand), and it scares most of us. You would think, being a person of faith and believing in a more beautiful eternity to come, that we would be excited to depart from this world. But there is still the fear of not knowing when, how or what it will feel like. Will it be quick and painless, or will I suffer? Will I get a chance to say goodbye to my loved ones or just see them someday on the other side? I was tormented with a lot of worries concerning these details until, again, I chose to remember that God is in control and knows every day that He has ordained in each of our lives. Faith is consistently choosing to let go of the "what ifs," the "whys," and the "hows" and trusting that God is faithful enough to have all the details worked out. My favorite scripture to apply in every situation is Romans 8:28 (NIV), "That in all things God works for the good of those who love him, who have been called according to his purpose." Everything doesn't have to be good for us to trust that God is working it all for our good and even greater good in this world and for advancing His kingdom.

Fear is very real, just like the devil is real, but we have to remember that he is a liar. And we can stand steadfast in our faith because of the promises of God, which is the truth that ultimately sets us free from fear. I realize that sounds like a simple statement or maybe complex, but I understand how paralyzing and terrifying fear is because I have had to face it for so many days of my life. I have found that the thoughts you meditate on the most are the ones that are going to have the most power in your life, and we can choose to have positive, faith-filled ones. Over the years, I can say that as my faith grew, fear became less prominent. I have learned what my triggers are, how to deal with them more accurately and work through each one as they come.

Many things don't scare me as much as they used to, and now I can do most things without worrying about crippling fear. Fear isn't as big as it seems when you call its bluff. Trust me, it has one, and you have the power within you to overcome it, as well. I still do many things even when I feel afraid just so it doesn't gain a grip over my life again. Right now, as I am writing this, I am facing many worries and concerns. There are the fears of failure, success, accomplishing my dreams, not accomplishing my dreams; the list never ends. But I choose to do it afraid and stand in faith, knowing that everything will work out as it is meant to. And you can do the same!

Life Lessons

- Courage is not the absence of fear but doing that in which you fear despite feeling it.
- Your dreams are just on the other side of your fears, so don't give up.
- Great reward doesn't come without great risk. Take the risk; it is worth the reward.
- God is greater than your greatest fear, so put your trust in Him.
- You can take your thoughts captive instead of letting them take you captive.

- Nothing is possible without God, but with God, all things are possible.

Prayer: *Lord, we choose to cast all of our fears and anxieties upon You, for You care for us. Help us when we struggle with our faith in You by Your amazing grace. Amen.*

Declaration: *I am clothed with strength and dignity, and I laugh without fear of the future (Proverbs 31:25).*

CHAPTER 16

POWER OF PRAISE

"Your lovingkindness is better than life"
(Psalm 63:3, NKJV).

Many have heard the saying that if you play a country song backwards, you get your spouse back, your house back, your dog back; you get the point. Well, I believe that when you praise God, you will get so much more in return. This is because God is in the business of redeeming and restoring. In the midst of my major depression in 2011, a friend of mine handed me a book called *Prison to Praise* by Merlin Carothers. It was one of the smallest but most powerful books I have ever read. He revealed the one solution to every single problem in our life. Seriously, one simple thing you can do to fix all of your problems? Can you imagine that? Are you ready for the answer that will change your life? It's the power of praise. You may skeptically reply with, "Really, how is that the answer to all of life's problems?" Well, I believe it is, too, and I will share why.

Now, I love to sing praise and worship songs. Whether I am in my car, the living room or church, it doesn't matter where I praise God as long as I do. The praises of my heart go forth continually in songs, words, thoughts, and even actions. Regardless of how you choose to do it, praise releases the Holy Spirit's power into your spirit, your heart, your mind and your life. I do not believe any other power we have available works better than declaring your praises to our Almighty God. Praising God for all things and in all situations is the highest stance in the spiritual realm as we humble ourselves with gratitude. God's anointing is readily available through praise, and it is the most powerful act of spiritual warfare. I am a fan of anything I can do that scares the devil away from my life and my loved ones and invites God's miraculous power to work divinely on my behalf.

Now, it almost sounds selfish to combine worshipping God along with our own desires, but that is what we really are: selfish human beings always wanting to know what is in it for us. This is called the great exchange, and praise is one of the greatest exchanges we can make. Jesus exchanged His life for ours, His righteousness for our sin and His salvation for our judgment. We already have God's love, so we praise Him. We already have His mercy, so we praise Him. We already have His favor, so we praise Him. This is all praiseworthy in itself. Yet, He has so much more to offer, even though He has already given us more than we possibly deserve.

Of course, in my frailty and forgetfulness, even after learning this most invaluable information, I still fail to realize this should be my first response when dealing with all of my own circumstances. In my pride and self-reliance, I tend to think that I have to try to solve all my own problems before bothering God with them, and then, only after exhausting all of my other options, I remember that He probably has a better way. I find myself complaining during tough times or struggling with my weaknesses before I remind myself that I have direct access to the one Source that provides every resource. I know there is power in prayer and claiming the promises of God, but we may not know how much power is in praising Him. Did you know that eagles not only fly above the storms they encounter, but they also use the winds of that storm to gain altitude and rise even higher? Praising God is like that in which not only can we ride out the storms of our life, but we can actually let them raise us even higher than we were before. Nothing on Earth will lift you above your problems more than the power of praise.

There are so many reasons why I am encouraged to praise God for everything. Most importantly, it is our humble acknowledgment that He is God and we are not. He is in control of everything, and He uses it all to fulfill His purposes: the good, the bad and the ugly. He is the Creator, and we are His creation. He holds the entire universe in His hands, including our very being. He knows what you need and don't need in every given situation. He knows your past, present and future. He knows how to arrange and rearrange things in such a way that not only benefits you but so many others around you. He is all-knowing (omniscient), all-sufficient (omnipresent) and all-powerful (omnipotent).

Therefore, we cannot fully comprehend the impact that praise brings into our lives. Otherwise, we would spend most of our time on our knees or standing with our arms lifted high in awe and gratitude. Trust me, I am preaching to myself as well right now. And praise opens up the heavenly realm on our behalf. There is truly a supernatural power released when we praise God. Not only do we scare the devil and his demonic minions from our presence, but it draws God's heart ever so close to ours. The closest comparison I can put into human terms is that it is one of the most passionate and intimate forms of love that we can express to our Creator, our first love. If you have never felt connected to God, praise Him and let His warm presence encompass you unlike any human ever could. Worship is not merely singing but more of a heart posture, letting the words of humility and gratitude flow from your lips and entire soul.

Because God is love, He loves you and wants you to fully believe that He is worthy of all the glory that He possesses. The Bible tells us that the eyes of the Lord search the whole earth for people who have given their hearts completely to Him. Praise grabs His attention, and He blesses us abundantly more than we can even imagine when we lean on and trust in Him. One of the amazing advantages I have found when praising God is that it completely takes my focus off of myself and my problems and puts the focus on Him. It is so powerful that my attitude is instantly transformed because there is something so much better to focus on than my problems. The prophet Isaiah says that God gives us the garment of praise for the spirit of heaviness.

So, whether I am immersed in the blissful feelings of love or the heartache of pain, I can praise God. Whether my bank account has sufficient or insufficient funds, I can praise God. If I am sick or feeling well, I can praise God. When I am struggling with an addiction or standing free on the mountaintop, I can praise God. Regardless if I am walking in the light, surrounded by darkness or wandering in the wilderness, I can praise God. If you are facing the heartbreak of divorce, you can praise God. If your daughter is entrapped in an abusive relationship, you can praise God. If your son is addicted to drugs, you can praise God. If you have more debt than you have income, you can praise God. If you are so depressed that death seems like the next best option, you can praise God. If you are diagnosed with a terminal disease, you can praise God. We can praise God in every situation and for every situation.

I totally understand that it would seem absurd to thank God for the horrible things that we or our loved ones go through and can feel very uncomfortable, but that is only in our flesh. However, in the spiritual realm, this is where miracles take place. This is where God's super meets our natural and supernatural things can occur. For His thoughts are not our thoughts, and His ways are not our ways, and we may not know what the outcome will be, but He does. He can do in your life what He did for Martha and Mary when He raised their brother from the grave three days after his death. He may allow everything to be taken away like Job and then restore twice what was lost. Or, He may take the life of your child as He did with David's son, who then washed himself and worshipped God even though he did not get the answer he prayed for. What an amazing testament. If only we would be so sold out to God to give Him the same honor and glory that these men and women did.

Hallelujah is the most glorious singular word used in the heavens, and there is no greater word proclaimed there.

There are many scriptures throughout the Bible that reveal even the angels in heaven are singing, praising and worshipping God. Did you know that man was created just lower than angels, yet Paul says that we will judge the angels? Did you know that angels have free will, just like us? Otherwise, Lucifer would not have been able to convince one-third of them to go with him when he was cast out of heaven. So, I think that it is worth noting that if the angels, who are higher than us and can actually see God in His highest glory, would choose by their own will to worship and praise the Most High, maybe we should take the same position. Someday, we will be alongside the angels worshipping God for all eternity, so we might as well get a good start here and now.

One day, as I was ministering to a friend of mine who was struggling with some unexpected challenges, God brought to my remembrance the power of praise that He had recently revealed to me. From my spirit, I felt led to write this letter of praise on her behalf. She was so encouraged and uplifted at that moment that she praised God and chose to trust Him with the situation. And you are free to use it as a guide to start praising Him for whatever you are facing right now.

Dear Lord, we praise You for the work You are doing in and for us. We thank You for Your awesome plan of salva-

tion. We praise You for the sacrifice of Your perfect Son so that we may be found perfect in Your sight. We thank You for allowing us to fall into any pit so that we may see Your mighty hand lift us out. We praise You that You have the victory, and we claim it as our inheritance. We thank You that You created us for Your own purpose. We praise You that You will finish the good work You started. We thank You that we will continue to stumble into Your perfect will and plan for us, regardless of our own mistakes. Thank You for so perfectly loving us in the midst of our imperfection. We praise You for allowing every situation into our life, knowing that it is only You that can and will be glorified with each victory. We cast every fear and anxiety onto You, for You did not give us a spirit of fear or confusion but of a sound mind. May Your peace surpass all logic and human understanding. We praise Your mighty name and worship only You. By the power of the blood of Jesus Christ, we proclaim all goodness shall follow us all the days of our lives. Amen.

Just rereading that lifts my spirit and encourages me to worship God in the midst of all of my own hopes, dreams, worries and concerns. The very popular scripture found in Philippians 4:6–7 (NKJV) (emphasis added by the author) says, Be anxious for nothing, but in *everything* by prayer and supplication, with *thanksgiving*, let your requests be made known to God;

and the peace of God, which surpasses all understanding, will guard your hearts and minds through Christ Jesus.

I italicized the words "everything" and "with thanks-giving" so we don't miss that part. And this confirms the great exchange. We exchange our anxiety for His peace, our worries for gratitude and our troubles for His care and guardianship.

Life Lessons

- We praise God in all things and for all things because He is God. Period.
- Praise is an act of confession that we are humbly and gratefully awestruck by the power and majesty of our Creator.
- We can cast our cares and worries on God, tap into the power of prayer and worship and trust Him to do the miracles that only He can do. This is why He gets all the glory.
- Praise is the most powerful weapon in the spiritual realm and disarms the enemy. The battle is real, and we are all called to be warriors.

Prayer: *Lord, thank You that You are worthy to be praised and worshipped in and for every situation and that* *because of Your great mercy, Your supernatural power works on our behalf. Amen.*

Declaration: *I continually offer God the sacrifice of praise through Jesus Christ, giving thanks to His name (Hebrews 13:15).*

CHAPTER 17

SWEET SURRENDER

"Because He first loved us" (1 John 4:19, NKJV).

In 2 Timothy 3, we are warned that in the last days, people would be lovers of themselves, lovers of money and lovers of pleasure rather than lovers of God. Now, Paul preached this with urgency almost 2000 years ago that we were already living in the last days, yet, here we still are. Although, we do not have to look very far to see that the world is rapidly decaying and preparing for the return of our Messiah. With the advancement of technology and materialism, the abounding acceptance of immorality, as well as an overgrowing population, most of us would not argue that we may be in the last of the last days. However, only Jesus knows exactly where we are on His timeline.

We live in an era where the common mentality is what's in it for me and instant gratification, and I, too, struggle with this myself much of the time. It's really part of our nature from birth. By toddler age, we are already screaming about what is ours and not wanting to share our toys. As we get older, hopefully, we will learn how Jesus was the perfect example of a surrendered life. He was never about His own will. Even though He experienced human feelings of hunger and pain, He chose to be obedient to His Father's will. How much better would we be, and the world, if we lived with that same mindset? Looking back at my own life and the world around me, I can see where choosing our own will and desires has caused great havoc and consequences; we hurt others, we hurt ourselves and we hurt God.

There was no greater example of surrender in human history than what Jesus did for us. It was out of complete obedience and sacrifice that He endured the excruciating death on a cross to save each one of us. However, He did not just come to die but also to show us how to live. Jesus' example of His relationship with God is a reflection of the relationship God wants with us. Sometimes, we may think that we do not deserve to have a genuine and loving relationship with God because of our own shortcomings or that His love is only reserved for those who are good enough. But the truth is that God loves you in your imperfect condition just as much as He loves His perfect Son... just as much!

The Scriptures put it so beautifully that we simply love Him because He first loved us and that, while we were yet sinners, Christ died for us. You can see that, in most of my past, I was used, abused and taken advantage of. All I ever wanted was to be loved, only to be rejected, abandoned or let down much of the time. Thankfully, I have found the One who truly loves me and who will never leave nor forsake me. No matter how many walls I put up or try to hide behind, His love always finds me. After looking back over forty years of my life, I know God never did anything to hurt me; it was broken people who did that. And in my brokenness, I hurt many others. But He never once turned His back on me; it was I who turned away from Him. Countless times, I ran from Him in my pride, rebellion and shame. But He was always tugging at my heart until I would come running back, and He gave me a safe place in His arms to fall.

Any other image of God is distorted, and we are deceived if we think we are not loved by Him for any reason. We cannot even fathom the depth of His love for us. Part of our issue is that we believe that He loves as the world loves. But the world is self-centered and full of conditions. God's love is unconditional. I've heard many Christians exclaim that biblically, His love has many conditions, but it doesn't. Maybe some of our blessings are conditional, yet He is still generous in even that. I am living proof of the extent of both His love and blessings, for when I was the most unlovable, He showed me even more grace and mercy. And every blessing I received, I did not earn or deserve. And until we realize this, we cannot truly love ourselves and others. God does not look at us through our struggles the same way we look at ourselves or other people's. Where we see weakness, He sees His strength; where we see loss, He sees redemption; where we see failure, He makes a victory. Some beautiful truths from the Bible tell us that where sin abounds, grace abounds more (Romans 5:20). That absolutely nothing can separate us from the love of God (Romans 8:38–39). And whoever is forgiven much loves much (Luke 7:47).

When God asks us to surrender to His love and His will, it is not so that He can take anything away from our lives but so that He can give us so much more. Jesus, knowing what He had to go through, would do it again because He knew there was a greater purpose intended: saving the people He loves, which includes you and me. Jesus completely surrendered His own life in order to save ours. This is the example of perfect love. Thankfully, by God's grace and mercy, death and defeat was not the end of His story but just the beginning of a new one. Death was defeated when Jesus arose three days later, and salvation became available to all people. When we study His life, we see the sacrifice and beauty of surrender. He who was Most High became the lowest of all, and the Almighty King became a servant for the sake of rebuilding His own kingdom. And in this, we are shown how much we are loved and how to love others.

When Jesus asks us to lay down our life for Him, it is after He has already chosen to lay His life down for us. He has a greater purpose for our lives, and we will not know what that is until we choose to surrender to Him. And yet, with this knowledge, we still ask what is in it for us. Well, we already got everything we need and more than we deserve, so our motive should no longer be to give in order to receive but to give because we have already received. True, surrendering at times will seem inconvenient, unfair and unjust because it may cost us something initially, but the return is so much more than we could ever invest.

The Bible says in Luke 17:33 that those who try to save their own life will lose it, and those who choose to lose it for Him will find it. Again, we see that the biblical principles are the opposite of the world's. Instead of the concept that the more we hold onto for ourselves, the more we will have; it's the more that we give away, the more abundant life we will gain. And the truth is, the more we store up for ourselves, even that will be taken away.

I finally learned this lesson in my own life when I was forty-two years old and finally started tithing on all the money I earned. I grew up in the church, so I know what the Bible says about giving the firstfruits of our income, but because I struggled with the fear of not having enough for myself and my family, I justified not to. I felt the Holy Spirit working in my heart in this area and prompting me to trust Him with my money. I was not feeling led by religious rules but by a nudge that God wanted me to learn to trust Him in yet another area of my life. Sure, I can give Him my time, my attention and my heart, but my money? That was a little too much risk for a single girl trying to make it in this economy. However, God had recently given me a very affordable apartment in the area that I loved and provided me with a job that allowed me to work part-time and still fully support myself financially.

As I looked around and saw all that He had already provided, along with Him insistently asking me to start tithing, I knew it was not because He needed my money but because He wanted to show me His faithfulness. Plus, I realized that I was possibly limiting all that He wanted to do for me because I was withholding my trust from Him. So, I committed to giving ten percent of all my income every week. I gave a part of the money I earned at work, side jobs and even received as gifts. It didn't matter where the money came from, I included it all. Immediately, financial abundance started pouring in. People would randomly give me money, my work started giving me bonus checks almost every week that were as much as my normal paychecks would be if I was still working full-time. I was astonished, ecstatic and a little bummed that I had not trusted Him so much sooner.

I am so grateful for the life I now have. I work only two days a week in an office, bring in extra income from fast-food deliveries when I need to and have plenty of time and energy to grow in my relationship with God, enjoy time with loved ones and pursue my dreams. I live on my own and have more than enough to completely support myself. God clearly showed me that I can trust Him with every aspect of my life. The more I give to Him, the more He provides for me. And I don't do anything to get something back, but because He is faithful, He takes care of me. God is saying to you today: Trust Me and watch what I will do. He can do more in a short period of time than we could accomplish on our own in an entire lifetime.

The definition of surrender is to cease resistance to an enemy or opponent and submit to their authority. The thing is, God is not our enemy, nor tries to be an opponent. Satan is the real enemy, and yet, we are so willing to submit to him, even unintentionally, through deception. Romans 6:16 says we are either a slave to sin or a slave to righteousness; whichever we surrender to becomes our master. We may think that we have authority over ourselves, but this is not completely true. It's like how freedom isn't free because it does cost something. I know when I give in to the ways of this world or my own temptations, my life is full of chaos and confusion; nothing within me is truly satisfied or fulfilled. There is never enough when it comes to our flesh, and it will always want more no matter how much we give it: more food, more drugs, more sex, more attention, etc.

However, the times when I submit to God, the complete opposite is true. My fleshly desires cease; I only want more of God, and He fills my heart and spirit to overflowing. I am more than satisfied, sometimes to the point of being overwhelmed and cannot handle anymore. The more of Himself that He pours into my life, the more overflow I have to bless those around me. His light fills my soul and radiates for all to see, and He receives all the glory. Just before Jesus went to the cross, He looked up to heaven and asked for glory to be given to Him so that glory would go back to God. The more we are willing to surrender, the more tremendous work God can do in our lives, and then He will be even more glorified. This is where we find the meaning and purpose for our life, and God can use us to impact the world around us. Ephesians 3:20 says He can do more than we could ever ask, think or imagine.

Life Lessons

- Control and surrender are both equally difficult, but one leads to life and the other to death.
- God opposes the proud but gives grace to the humble. Surrender is simply swallowing our pride and humbling ourselves unto our Almighty God.
- God has good plans for those who are willing to surrender to His will, not to harm you but to give you a hope and a future.
- El Shaddai is one of God's names in Hebrew, meaning "more than enough." He is faithful to give you all that you need and still bless you with so much more.

Prayer: *Lord, remind us of the meekness we find in Jesus as He surrendered to You, and help give us the strength and desire to do the same. Amen.*

Declaration: *I follow Jesus daily by denying myself and taking up my cross (Luke 9:23).*

CHAPTER 18

REPENT–JESUS IS COMING!

"For God so loved the world that He gave His only begotten Son" (John 3:16, NKJV).

Oh, the glorious day that so many of us, and all the generations before, are looking forward to. The moment when the trumpet will sound for all the nations to hear and the sky is split open to reveal the full glory of Jesus Christ coming down on a cloud with His army of angels. His imminent return is a promise He made when He ascended into heaven from Earth the first time He was here. The very last words of Jesus were written at the end of Revelation, stating, "Surely I am coming quickly" (Revelation 22:20, NKJV). I understand that our patience is growing weary after waiting nearly 2000 years, but we must remember that time is not measured the same way in heaven as it is on earth. In fact, they say that one day in heaven is like 1000 days on Earth, so I often state that it's really just been a long weekend for Jesus since He left. However, there is no denying that with each passing day, we only draw closer to His return.

I believe there is no better time than now to turn to God

for His saving grace. As I have testified, and hopefully, you can see, God is a redeemer, restorer and healer. Regardless of your circumstances, whether you suffered at the hands of your adversaries or your own poor choices, God can change you and the outcome of your life, now and for eternity. However, the only way to allow Him to save us is to humble our hearts, repent for our sins and surrender to His perfect love and will.

The word repent is often misunderstood and, sometimes, debatable regarding exactly what it means and how we accomplish it. Some believe it is an actual turning away from sin and changing the direction of your life back to God. Others believe it is merely the feeling of regret or remorse for their sinful behavior. And then there are those who believe it means to simply change your mind about what you believe. Well, according to Webster's dictionary, all three perspectives are correct. Nevertheless, all of them can be very challenging to achieve, especially as it is explained in the Bible about us being in the end times because many hearts have become so hard and deceived by the world.

It has already been prophesied that we will go through very troubling times, and many will fall away from their faith. But that does not mean that you or I have to be one of them. The door is still open right now for us to change our minds, our hearts and our direction. God is patiently waiting for us to come back to Him. The good news for believers and the bad news for those who do not believe in God's truth is that no matter what, Jesus is coming back. Regardless of our differences in experiences, opinions or beliefs, we will all come face to face with the Messiah of the world one day. He will bring with Him reward for those who followed Him and judgment for those who did not, simple as that.

Whether a believer of Christ or an enemy of His Word, in that moment, every knee will bow, and every tongue will confess that Jesus Christ is Lord. I don't know about you, but when He shows up that day, I want to be one that He claims is His. So, how do we get the assurance that we will be united with God and reunited with our loved ones who went before us? Well, the most popular scripture about our salvation is written in John 3:16 (NKJV), "For God so loved the world that He gave His only begotten Son, that whoever believes in Him shall not perish but have everlasting life." Then, Romans 10:9 (ESV) states that "if you confess with your mouth that Jesus is Lord and believe in your heart that God raised him from the dead, you will be saved." The Bible makes it so clear and simple that all we have to do is believe in Him, and we shall live. This is the greatest promise and gift ever given to us.

It is not Jesus plus good works, Jesus plus striving for perfectionism, Jesus plus following the law; it is only Jesus Christ, who died on a cross and was then resurrected from death, that saves us. Our salvation is by faith alone, and that is it, and for a few very important reasons. Jesus is the only human being yet God in the flesh who was perfect and acceptable to be the atoning sacrifice for all of the world, once and for all. If His bloodshed did not cover the penalty for sin in full, then it would have all been done in vain, and there would be no victory to cling to. He was and is the ultimate and final sacrifice to fully satisfy God's wrath that we deserved due to our sinful nature.

Secondly, if our salvation was contingent on any of our works, we would not be able to testify about the abundance of God's grace and mercy. Paul clearly explains in Ephesians 2:8–9 (NIV) that salvation is a gift from God, through faith, and not works, so that none of us can boast. Lastly, the Bible tells us that none of us, not even one, is righteous (Romans 3:10), that even our greatest works are just as good as filthy rags (Isaiah 64:6) and that breaking just one commandment makes us just as guilty as breaking them all (James 2:10). These are beautiful scriptures because it humbles us, reminds us that we cannot strive to be good enough and reveals our need for a Savior. The good news is that God sent us Jesus Christ.

Now that we have been offered this new covenant of grace, what now? Can we just do whatever we want? Does it matter if we continue sinning since our salvation cannot be earned and, therefore, cannot be lost? The powerful thing about grace is that not only are we able to be free from the punishment of sin, but we can also be free from the bondage of sin. We are told that whom the Son sets free is free indeed (John 8:36), yet we are either a slave to sin or a slave to righteousness (Romans 6:16). It sounds kind of contradictory that we can be free and slaves at the same time but the point is that whichever we serve becomes our master. We have the freedom to follow our flesh, which causes sin and leads to death (spiritually), or we can follow Christ, which leads to life (eternally).

I once heard somebody say that when they are not regularly communicating with God, they don't feel guilty; they feel thirsty. This is the difference between religion and a relationship with God. Our soul was created for an intimate relationship with our Creator. Jesus came to bring us back into that perfect relationship with our Heavenly Father, not just another religion. Thankfully, we do not have to walk this out with our own willpower and strength. Jesus sent His Holy Spirit to live within us, guide us into His truth and enable us to walk in victory.

First of all, the truth for all of us is that God loves each one of us, even those who do not believe in Him. And because of His love for us, He wants us to love ourselves and to love others. God created us from His very finger, breathed His life in us and now His Spirit is available to live within us. If we fail to realize the power of the Holy Spirit, we will continue to struggle. I know I would have no hope if I did not have an all-powerful, all-loving God to put my faith in and be the foundation of my life. Everything in our world is temporal and fleeting, including our physical bodies, so we have nothing other than Jesus to firmly grasp onto. I understand that it sounds simple, or maybe complex, to trust in something or someone that we cannot see with our own eyes. But the spiritual eyes of our faith bring us into a deeper presence that we may not see but can feel deep within our being.

Not too long ago, I found out that my grandpa was a writer, as well. Maybe this gift is a generational blessing. He is now in his late nineties, still going strong and absolutely loves the Lord. I believe his faith is a generational blessing, too. Years ago, he wrote an article on how we get into heaven, and I could not put it in better words myself. So, with his permission, I will share with you the revelation that God gave to him.

Since God is a God of justice as well as a God of love, He had to do something. Since sin and death cannot co-ex-

ist with God, He had to bridge the gap somehow—the gap that stood between His love and His justice. That gap was bridged by a blood sacrifice. In order for you to have your sins forgiven by God, you have to bring a blood sacrifice, right? This was the criterion in the Old Testament. The criterion for today is not what we bring but what we receive. God is offering His own sacrifice, His only begotten Son, and whoever believes in Him will have everlasting life. This gift of God's love is so overwhelming; it is hard to believe that anyone would not want to receive it. And receiving Christ assures you of eternal life. Jesus said I am the way, the truth and the life; no one comes to the Father except through Me.

So, it's all up to you whether or not you will go to heaven. Going to heaven is based upon what you do with Jesus Christ and not upon what kind of a person you are or what kind of a life you have lived. Many people think that if they go to church and give their time, money and talents, are good to others or don't do any really bad stuff, they will get into heaven. The question then arises: how do you accept Him? Well, how do you accept a birthday or Christmas gift? You simply reach out with your hands and say, "Thank you." With the gift of salvation, it's the same way, except you reach out with your heart and say to Him, "Thank You" for filling the void that's been there all of your life.

Accepting Christ into your heart simply means believing that Christ completed the work of salvation on your behalf. Salvation is a gift. It is free, to us, that is. But it sure cost God plenty in giving up His only begotten Son just for us. So, who do you think you are rejecting the most precious gift God wants to give you? First Corinthians 15:1–3 tells us just what we are to believe that Christ died for our sins, was buried and rose again on the third day according to the scriptures; He was seen by many people as proof of His resurrection. He died so that we may live eternally. Read John 3:16 (NKJV) and put your name in place of the word "whoever." "For God so loved the world that He gave His only begotten Son, that [your name] believes in Him should not perish but have everlasting life."

In Titus 2:11, we are told that the grace of God has been revealed, bringing salvation to all people; "all people" includes you and me. Are you ready to receive your life-giving gift of eternal salvation? Do you want an intimate relationship with your Heavenly Father, who is longing for your return and to embrace you with open arms? Do you want to meet Jesus Christ as the Savior and Redeemer of your soul? And do you want to be filled with the power of the Holy Spirit, the same power that resurrected Jesus Christ from the grave? If you said yes to the abundant life that Jesus is so eagerly ready to give you, just repeat the prayer below. You can say it out loud or silently in your heart; God hears it all.

Dear Lord, I thank You for the free gift of salvation that cost me nothing but for You, cost Your very life. I know that it is not the work of my flesh but only by the finished work of the cross that I am saved. I receive Jesus Christ as my personal Lord and Savior and declare that His blood covered all of my sins: past, present, and future. I believe that it is only through the death of Your Son that I shall live eternally with You. Please fill me with the power of Your Holy Spirit so that I may be guided into Your truth all the days of my life. In the powerful name of Jesus Christ, amen.

Congratulations! I am so blessed to now call you my brother or sister in Christ. If I do not get to meet you in this lifetime, I will get to meet you in heaven when we are all resurrected with our new glorified bodies in the presence of the Almighty Lord. I would encourage you to find fellow believers (Hebrews 10:25), get baptized (Acts 2:38) and start reading God's Word (Hebrews 4:12) to help you grow in your new spiritual journey. As part of the body of Christ, we are privileged to come together in prayer and worship of the Most High God. I will be praying for you to have the strength and courage to climb the mountains set before you and get through the valleys below. However-er, you are never alone, for God Himself goes before you, walks beside you and will never leave you. And, if at any time, the devil tries to convince you that you are not quali-fied for God's love, too far gone to be saved or in any way lost your salvation, remember that he is a liar.

Life Lessons

- Jesus is fully God and fully human. He has the power and authority of God, yet He felt all the same pain and temptations that we go through while He was on Earth.

- The life, death and resurrection of Jesus Christ were witnessed and written about throughout the Gospels found in the New Testament of the Bible. All the prophecies of the coming Messiah written in the Old Testament were fulfilled by Him and Him alone.

- God had a plan from the beginning when man first sinned, beginning with Adam and Eve. God's prom-ise came with the birth of Christ, and so shall His promise to return.

- The Father, Son and Holy Spirit are one deity fulfill-ing different roles of the same Godhead. Jesus Christ has been given all authority in Heaven and on Earth.

Prayer: *Lord, we thank You that You made a way for us through Your Son, Jesus Christ, to be reconciled with You now and for all of eternity. Amen.*

Declaration: *I believe in the good news of the salvation of Jesus Christ. I put my trust in Him alone, repent for my sins and have the power of the Holy Spirit to walk in victory every day (Mark 1:15; Acts 1:8).*

CHAPTER 19

LET YOUR LITTLE LIGHT SHINE

"Love never fails" (1 Corinthians 13:8, NKJV).

I definitely do not know everything about anything but only that which I have learned through my own experiences, foolishness or what God has revealed to me thus far. Everybody has a story. In fact, many of your stories could be just as or much more heartbreaking and tragic or amazing and powerful than mine. This is why I am so humbled and grateful that God chose to use my ordinary life to magnify Him in such an extraordinary way. Yet, I am only one in approximately 8 billion people currently on Earth, and God wants each of us to help reveal His glory by sharing what He has done in our lives. He has a great plan and purpose for everyone, and nothing He created was by accident or error. This is why Jesus left us with His greatest commandment and a great commission: to love your God with all your heart, mind and soul, to love others as yourself (Mark 12:30–31), and to go make disciples of all the nations (Matthew 28:19).

Sometimes, this sounds like a daunting and impossible task, and other times, it sounds like a daring adventure worth all the risks. I can attest that the times I chose to push past my fears, worries and doubts and follow the desires of my heart, God always met me there. Now, when I say follow my heart, that doesn't mean my fleshly desires, for the heart is the most deceptive and wicked above all things (Jeremiah 17:9). But these were the times when I stepped out in obedience to the Holy Spirit, believing there was a mission to fulfill just on the other side of my comfort zone and I had to use all my faith and courage to get there. We were not meant to follow the normalcies dictated by the world, staying complacent to what is familiar or comfortable. We are even warned that we are like sheep led to slaughter (Romans 8:36), but we have a Shepherd named Jesus Christ, who will never leave His flock; He may lead us on a path of uncertainty, yet He assures our victory.

Over time, I learned that even if I took a wrong turn or found myself at a dead end, God always had a way to get me back on track. Even when I allowed myself to be led astray or chased after the things of this world or my own desires, He was still able to turn my mess into a powerful message. When I was at my worst, His love for me was the greatest and brought me safely back to Him. This is the God of our universe, the Creator of Heaven and Earth. I no longer worry as much about making a mistake or fear when opposition comes, for that is part of our faith journey, and we never learn the lesson without going through it. Paul even tells us that we can rejoice in our sufferings because it produces endurance, which produces character, which produces hope (Romans 5:3–4).

Sometimes, I am like a moth that has been drawn to the flames of a fire, only to get burned. Many times, I just found myself in a situation where the only choice I had was to either sink or swim, so I chose to swim. And sometimes, I just had to learn how to tread water. Life is much like being in a lake. In one moment, you are just having a good time splashing around by the shoreline, then you find that you've drifted out above your head, and you need Jesus to grab your hand to pull you back out. No matter what, you will be okay because our Savior walks on water and will never let you go. I do not take credit for how far I have come in my journey, as I was just desperate many, many times for God to save me. I am eternally grateful that He did, over and over, and I know that He will continue to do so.

For the past forty-five years, God has clung to me, and many times, I have clung to Him. I believed way back in my late twenties that God had something great for me to do. It was like a knowing deep within my spirit that I could never shake, no matter how much I feared or doubted the possibilities. Then, twelve years ago, in my darkest moment, He gave me a glimpse of this book. Over those next several years, God showed up in so many miraculous ways to keep me pressing forward, renew my hope and not completely give up. He has encouraged me along the way by using great men and women of faith to prophesy over my future and the ministry God has prepared me for that lined up with the desires, visions and dreams that have been tucked away in my heart for so long. A few weeks before finalizing this manuscript for the publisher, I prayed to God for a miracle and to show up more real than He ever has before; not like He hasn't done enough already, but I knew I needed more healing.

Two days later, my cousin showed up unexpectedly at my door; I didn't even know she knew where I lived since we only talked a few times a year at most. But she said God sent her with a message and that He saw all my pain and didn't want me carrying it anymore. I broke down in tears, and even now, as I write this, my eyes well up. She has been in ministry for many years, growing in her prophetic gift, and had just come back from a spiritual deliverance conference. She believed that I was under some demonic oppression, and I agreed that there were probably a few doors I had opened to the enemy. A couple of days later, I met her at her house, and we sat in her little prayer room. We took authority over any demonic spirits that seemed to have an influence and cast them out in the name of Jesus. I figured there were a few, but more and more kept showing up as we prayed for them to be revealed. I felt like we had cast out a whole legion of them by the time we were done. All of a sudden, I saw a vision: a black hole that appeared to have taken all these evil spirits and swallowed them up, and then it just closed up. Then, I saw a wound over my heart as if God had just done open heart surgery, so He stitched it up. Then I saw the stitches heal, and there was a scar left in its place. Immediately after that, I saw the scar disappear as if there had never been a wound at all. I felt so free!

I hadn't realized the full impact of this scenario and vision until a few weeks later. I was already ecstatic and continued in my freedom but dreaded having to reread my story all over again from the beginning. I could never get through the first few chapters without dread and darkness filling my mind and emotions, even to the point of wanting to jump out of a window. But this time, I felt absolutely nothing. I had no pain left associated with my past, whether something happened thirty days or thirty years ago. God did it! He completely healed me, and I don't even have a scar.

It reminds me of the story in Daniel 3 when King Nebuchadnezzar bound up and threw Shadrach, Meshack and Abednego into a fiery furnace, but instead of getting burned up, they saw all three men loosed, walking around inside the furnace, along with a fourth man that looked like the Son of God. The king ordered the men to come out of the furnace since they did not die, they were not burned, not a hair on their head or clothing was scorched, nor did they even smell of smoke. What a testimony we have in God! No burns, no scars, no wounds; completely whole and healed.

What about you? Your life is like a movie, except that it is real and not made up by Hollywood. It has its own script, and you play a critical role in every detail. Even though God is the Director who oversees all the production, you are part of the cast. When the camera is rolling, what do you want people to see, hear and feel from the storyline you are creating? Most importantly, what message do you want to send to your audience? How do you want your story to end? Do you want people hanging on to the edge of their seats when it appears the bad guy is going to win and you have no chance of victory, but, unexpectedly, you get back up and arise as the champion? The great news is that even if we lose some battles, God has already won the war. Through Jesus Christ, we fight from victory, not for victory. I already know how I want my story to end when I get to meet Jesus face to face and hear Him say,

"Well done, good and faithful servant" (Matthew 25:21, NIV).

Now, I truly love my life and myself just the way I am, with all my flaws, quirks and shortcomings. I am fascinated by how far God has brought me, and I am so glad that I never gave up. I would not take anything away from my story. It was through the darkest hours and the hardest moments that I grew the most. Besides, if it had all been perfect, this would be a very boring book to read. I totally understand Helen Keller when she says that life is either a daring adventure or nothing. She was a remarkable woman who did not need her eyesight to have great vision. In your life, you will laugh and you will cry, but the best times are when you laugh so hard that you cry.

If we can learn anything from the apostle Paul, it is acknowledging that even though we have not arrived, we choose to forget what lies behind us and reach forth to what is ahead. Remind yourself that even though the sun sets every night, it will arise the next morning. Until then, by God's abundant grace and mercy, the sun will illuminate the moon just enough so that we can still find our way through the dark. Don't be afraid to be the one that shines, even just a little bit, because it only takes a small night light to dispel the darkness in an entire room. So, my brothers and sisters, choose to live today like it is your last, laugh because it upsets the devil and love without expecting anything in return.

Life Lessons

- You will never regret putting your trust in Jesus. Life is going to have trials and tribulations, whether you believe in God or not, but it is so much more rewarding with Him.

- This life is so temporary and short, even if we live a hundred years, but eternity is forever. You can secure your future now by accepting Jesus Christ as your personal Lord and Savior; He is waiting for you.

- God is love, and He loves you, no matter what you think or have done. Like a loving Father, He wants what is best for you and has a great inheritance available.

- Hurting people hurt people, but healed people help others heal. Let Jesus heal your heart, mind and soul, and then go proclaim to the world what He has done.

- Jesus is coming back. We don't know when, but we will all face Him on the day of judgment. Some will be praising His glory, and others will be trembling with fear. Choose today whom you will serve.

Prayer: *Lord, we thank You for Your Word and Your truth so that we may be used as a light in this dark world. Continually remind us that we were made to be loved and share Your love. Amen.*

Declaration: *I am the salt and the light of the world, and others will see my good works and glorify my Heavenly Father (Matthew 5:13–16).*

OTHER BOOKS RECOMMENDED BY SHAWNA MARTIN

Living Beyond Your Feelings by Joyce Meyer

Battlefield of the Mind by Joyce Meyer

The Confident Woman by Joyce Meyer

How to Hear from God by Joyce Meyer

The Bondage Breaker by Neil T. Anderson

Freedom from Fear by Neil T. Anderson

Demons and Spiritual Warfare by Ron Phillips

Prison to Praise by Merlin Carothers

Destined to Reign by Joseph Prince

The Five Love Languages by Gary Chapman

No Place to Cry by Doris Van Stone and Erwin W. Lutzer

Depression by Don Baker and Emery Nester

Knowing God's Secrets by John Hunter

Beautiful Things Happen When a Woman Trusts God by Sheila Walsh

Boundaries by Dr. Henry Cloud and Dr. John Townsend

The Power of a Praying Wife by Stormie Omartian

Heaven Is for Real by Todd Burpo

90 Minutes in Heaven by Don Piper

God Never Blinks by Regina Brett

Attitude is Everything by Jeff Keller

The Emotionally Healthy Leader by Peter Scazzero

Who Switched Off My Brain? by Dr. Caroline Leaf

S.H.A.P.E. by Erik Rees

Never Abandoned by LoriJo Schepers

The Verbally Abusive Relationship by Patricia Evans

Emotional Blackmail by Susan Forward

Everybody, Always by Bob Goff

The 40-Day Sugar Fast by Wendy Speake

The Exchange by Karrie Garcia

The Easy Way to Quit Smoking by Allen Carr